Book Cover by SW Global Publishing (Pty) Ltd
Editing by SW Global Publishing (Pty) Ltd

Photographs by Joe Brooks Photography

Image: Cardinal by Patrice Bouchard

First edition

ISBN: 978-0-6452371-3-9

Holiday Memories Made with Every Cup

OUR JOURNEY CONTINUES

LEILA & ERIKA SHANOFF

DEDICATION

To our beloved Charlotte who we think about always and miss daily! She is always in our hearts and thoughts, guiding us in all that we do. We never saw a cardinal up close and personal until the day that Charlotte passed. We came home from the tea room to see a beautiful red cardinal sitting on our rooftop. Charlotte is still watching over us with a keen eye and loads of wonderful wisdom and advice!

Twas the night before teatime
and all through the store,
amazing odors were brewing,
for all to come for!

Tea sandwiches were nestled
on tiered servers with care,
with scones on the first plate
and desserts also there!

With classes in baking, charcuterie
and more, our guests do crafts
to cherish and adore!

The prep work is done,
come one and come all.

To Erika's Tea Room for
your Holiday ball!

OUR JOURNEY CONTINUES

The long and winding road that leads you back to our door inspires us to continue what we love to do! Our mission that we choose to accept and grow is to continue making "Memories with Every Cup!" What's better than everyday memories - Holiday memories! In our family, Holiday memories strengthen the bond between Leila and her daughter Erika. This special bond extends to our teatime family and friends. Laughter is the glue that holds these friendships together.

Since we last communicated with our special friends and customers much has happened. They say that God doesn't give you more than you can handle. We say enough is enough! Should we start the story by singing "Memories" - they are beautiful and yet, they can be painful to remember, or easy to forget. We are always singing through the day and are ready to laugh at a moment's notice. This is what keeps us moving on. Sarcasm is our bread and butter. We can't take things too seriously!

We continue to grow and change in this post Covid environment. As we see a decline in tea room reservations, we see an increase in special themed event attendees. More power to all our teatime heroes. We are introducing a 3-day teatime retreat that entices all our tea enthusiasts and tea loving friends. We'll tell you about this in more detail later in the book. This is a very exciting enhancement to our existing repertoire.

The good news is despite any obstacles that arise, we are having a good time having beautiful tea sets made for us and creating new scone flavors to go along with them. Additionally, we are writing new themed murder mysteries and creating delicious recipes that enhance the themes. Our bi-annual naming of new scone flavors has brought out nationwide new scone flavor combinations for us to try and some will remain on the menu.

Our journey will never end. We love working together, laughing together, and thinking out our next steps together. By leaning on each other and all of our teatime friends, we have a great support system that keeps away the bad juju and enhances our reason for what we do. We play to our strengths - Leila shows everyone her Popeye muscles, from making scones and Erika shows everyone her bat wings from sitting on the computer all day. This is an indication that brains and brawn are needed for teatime success.

We are not done yet and we don't expect to be done anytime soon. We want you to come along for the ride. It may be bumpy but it will definitely be fun. Boredom not allowed, just pure enjoyment and especially good food, good friends, and good tea!

OUR NEED TO FEED CONTINUES WITH THE HOLIDAYS

Holiday memories around the world are associated with the special food served and bring people together with joy and tradition. Holiday foods are more than just delicious dishes on a plate; they carry deep meanings and tell stories that go back generations. We are connected to the past while bringing loved ones together. We share fascinating holiday foods and the stories behind them.

The next time swimming season comes around, remember, it is right after Holiday teatime at Erika's Tea Room. No worries, your bikini will still fit. When you drink tea with a Holiday meal there are little to no calories. We saw this written somewhere online, so it must be true! This is the gospel we live by. All tea drinkers have bikini ready bodies, don't they?

Let me ask you if you had to choose between being skinny or eating Leila's delicious scones for the rest of your life, which would you choose? Remember, you can always buy loose fitting pants on sale!

At Erika's Tea Room a clean plate is a happy plate! But we do have to go boxes to eat later! Leila's "Need to Feed" pressures her to overly feed everyone who enters our doors. When Erika creates a Holiday menu and gives it to Leila to review, Leila constantly adds on another savory item and another sweet dessert.

Leila can not follow a recipe to save her life, even if it was one of her own recipes. She starts out looking at the recipe and then changes it on a whim. Measurements are only a suggestion to Leila. She'll tell CeCe (her right hand in the kitchen), this looks like too much sugar or this will taste even better by adding this. We call it the shit-a-ron method of cooking and baking, a pinch of this, a tad of that, or a ton of something else. It all seems to work, though!

Charlotte was the same instinctual cook. She taught Leila everything she knows. None of which rubbed off on the next generation. It seemed to skip Erika. Charlotte was one of the best cooks, Leila loved her meals. The only downfall, Charlotte could not bake to save her life. Since she could not follow a recipe, Charlotte could not bake. To change a baked good recipe you need to make it over and over again so that you will know what you could change and what you couldn't change.

Leila's need to feed has expanded over the last couple of years. We have always been a fan of going big or going home. Leila simply can not let anyone leave the tea room hungry. Recently, Leila has increased her repertoire with so many new recipes that she wants to share with her guests. It gives her insurmountable pleasure to hear everyone's response to all the new treats.

SPECIAL DIETARY NEEDS, THINGS I DO NOT EAT AND NEVER EAT

Let's get back to basics. There are real food allergies and then there are foods you just don't like to eat!

Erika carefully develops unique menus for all of our Holiday celebrations and themed events. We want to know if people read the Special Menus we create for every themed event. Leila would like to add after the listed items being served – "Just Kidding! Tell me what you think we should be serving!" Instead, people arrive after all food preparation is completed and tell us – "I never eat mayonnaise, I have never eaten mayonnaise in my entire life!" or "I don't eat eggs, but I do eat egg salad!".

Erika asks every guest as they make a reservation – "Do you have any dietary or food restrictions or allergies?" We still get – "I'm lactose free, gluten free, or vegan, etc. when they are seated at the table." Leila wants to ask if they think she can wiggle her nose as Samantha the witch did and get the food switched to meet the customer's needs.

Just the other day a customer told Leila that she did not eat eggs. She further told Leila that she did not know where the eggs came from. Leila would have loved to tell her that she buys her eggs in the grocery store but instead told her that she laid them fresh that very morning – "You want them fresh, right?". Talking about fresh. . . The chickens are back, busy laying. If not, the poor chickens get all bottled up and could explode!

There are those customers that do not eat shellfish! There are so many great recipes that do include shellfish like crab, lobster or shrimp. By the way, tuna is not a shellfish! Wanting to elevate a Holiday table, Leila wanted to make a Shrimp and Asparagus Quiche. It was such a luscious addition to a Holiday Feast that Leila wants to share the recipe with you!

Leila thinks back to her childhood. No one had dietary needs back then. Everyone ate everything that was put in front of their face. In fact, parents punished you if you did not finish what was on your plate. There were not all these ailments. Doctors didn't blame all sicknesses on being heavy and the things you put into your mouth. Are we traumatized by food now?

Leila often wonders if it is the quality of the food in the grocery stores. We all heard about Mad Cow's Disease. Are the cows still mad? Lastly, if the cows are mad does it change the taste of their milk or cheese, etc.? If you give a cow a cookie, and of course a gallon of milk, they would definitely be much happier. Also, the Bird Flu Epidemic affected the chickens. What do you bring to a chicken that has the flu? Chicken Soup - no that's the silence of the chickens.

Erika hopes all is back to normal with our animal friends! She gets very upset thinking that her favorite foods will not be available for the Holidays. Erika puts all her requests for her favorite Holiday meals in early so that she can enjoy them throughout the Season.

Many years ago, really decades, Leila had an epiphany. Leila was determined to make a lobster dish, so Sheldon (Leila's husband and Erika's Father) was coerced into driving to Sheepshead Bay, Brooklyn to the Lobster Market. Leila picked a huge live lobster to take home and cook. On the way home, upon hearing rustling in the back seat, Leila started to scream, as the lobster started crawling out of the paper bag it was wrapped in. Sheldon drove across all lanes of the Belt Parkway until they were safely off the road and able to tie down the feisty crustation. Larry the Lobster spent the rest of the trip alone in the dark trunk!

And so, Larry the Lobster became the focus of the Feast of the Seven Fishes for our Holiday dinner. When Sheldon and Leila got home with Larry the Lobster, Leila was afraid to take him out of the bag. She was also afraid to take the rubber bands off of his large claws. Leila put the large stock pot with water to boil. She made Sheldon do all of the dirty work and finally put Larry into the pot for his hot water bath.

Leila believes that the tradition of the Feast of the Seven Fishes brings a special elevation to a Holiday celebration. This tasty treat is a way to take the best from the sea to the table. Ask any mermaid you happen to see what's the best seafood, everything from the sea! Leila's fondest childhood memories were at her Mom's table, eating all her favorite Holiday meals with family. Ah, Hearth and Home. Let's go back to how things used to be!

Shrimp and Asparagus Quiche Recipe

INGREDIENTS

2 12-ounce bags Steamable Asparagus

1-pound bag of Frozen Tail-on Extra Large Pre-cooked Shrimp

1 8-ounce package shredded Whole Milk Mozzarella Cheese

¼ cup dried Chives (can use fresh chopped Scallions instead)

10 large Eggs

1 32-ounce container of Heavy Cream

2 teaspoons of ground Black Pepper

2 teaspoons of Garlic Powder

2 teaspoons of Onion Powder

½ cup Bisquick Pancake and Baking Mix

DIRECTIONS

1. Heat oven to 375 degrees.
2. Line 2 muffin tins with parchment standard size liners.
3. Place the colander in the sink. Pull tail off frozen shrimp and put in the colander. Run cold water over shrimp until they are defrosted. Cut the shrimp into thirds. Set aside.
4. Steam asparagus for 6 minutes in the microwave. Let cool and cut into bite size pieces.
5. In a large bowl crack eggs and cream. Whisk until incorporated.
6. Add Spices and Bisquick. Whisk until smooth.
7. Add Shrimp, Asparagus, Chives and Cheese to the Egg Mixture. Stir thoroughly.
8. Spoon even amounts of mixture into the 24 muffin liners.
9. Bake for 15-20 minutes until golden brown.

Leila's Tasteful Tips:

- You can substitute Crab Meat for the Shrimp or add Crab Meat to make the quiche more succulent.
- Not a shellfish lover: Change the Shrimp to Chicken or Turkey.
- Change up the Mozzarella Cheese for a Sharp Cheddar or a Gruyere Cheese.

Feast of the Seven Fishes Seafood Salad in a Tortilla Bowl Recipe

INGREDIENTS FOR SEAFOOD SALAD

1.5 pound bag of frozen Seafood Medley (calamari, mussels, shrimp, and scallops)

1 8-ounce container of real lump Crab Meat

2 3.5-ounce Lobster Tails

1 10-ounce can whole Baby Clams

2 Vidalia Onions (peeled and diced)

1 of each - Green, Red and Yellow Peppers (cleaned and diced)

2 Tablespoons Canola Oil

1 ½ sticks salted Butter

¼ cup of Heavy Cream

2 teaspoons ground Black Pepper

2 teaspoons Garlic Powder

2 teaspoons Onion Powder

1 10.5-ounce can of condensed Cream of Celery Soup

DIRECTIONS FOR SEAFOOD SALAD

1. Fill a medium stock pot halfway with water. Bring to a boil.

2. Lower the heat to medium. Add the Lobster Tails and the Seafood Medley and simmer for 10 minutes. Drain and let cool.

3. Pull mussels out of the shells, the tails off the shrimp, and the lobster tails out of the shells. Chop up shrimp and lobster tails into bite size pieces.

4. Peel and dice the onions.

5. In a large frying pan, put oil and onions and put on high heat.

6. Clean and dice the 3 peppers.

7. After the onions are light brown, add the peppers to the frying pan of onions and continue to caramelize.

8. Add all the fishes to the pan.

9. Add the butter and continue to saute until all the seafood is tender.

10. Add the spices and mix in thoroughly.

11. Add the heavy cream and the condensed soup at the very end. When done, put equal amounts in the Tortilla Bowls and Serve.

INGREDIENTS FOR TORTILLA BOWL

8-inch Flour or Corn Tortillas

2 Tablespoons Vegetable Oil, or Canola Oil, or melted Butter

Cooking Spray

DIRECTIONS FOR TORTILLA BOWL

1. Preheat the oven to 375 degrees.

2. Brush oil on both sides of the tortillas.

3. Lightly spray the bottom of a 12-cup muffin tin with cooking spray.

4. Keeping the muffin tin upside down, push 4 tortillas in between the muffins on each corner to form the bowls.

5. Bake for 7 to 10 minutes until brown.

Leila's Tasteful Tips:

1. Instead of putting the seafood salad in a tortilla bowl, cook up a cup of brown rice and serve on top of the rice.

2. You can substitute any other fish for the 7 we listed above. Cod, Tilapia, or Halibut all work well with this recipe.

3. You can also use a different choice of condensed soup such as Cream of Onion or Cream of Asparagus. Additionally, you can add vegetables to the recipe to go along with the soup (asparagus or celery).

4. These tortilla bowls are so tasty you can use them for any filling (leftovers). If you want the tortilla bowls for fruit filling (with or without ice cream), brush them with melted butter and sprinkle with cinnamon sugar before baking them.

A CLEAN TEAROOM IS A HAPPY TEAROOM

Cleanliness is next to Godliness. We say that in Grandma Charlotte's house you could have eaten off the floor. We never saw a woman that cleaned her entire house daily. She washed her marble floors on her hands and knees. She hung out the second-floor windows cleaning them inside and out. Charlotte vacuumed her carpet every day and made sure there wasn't a footprint in sight. The vacuum lines had to go all in one direction or else it had to be redone.

No one was allowed to step foot in Charlotte's living room. Dark wine velvet carpet was on the floor. You couldn't step a toe in the living room without leaving a mark. As a young one Leila would put a footprint on the carpet to see how her Mom would react. She was the devil incarnate. On Leila's wedding day, she was finally allowed to enter this precious domain, footprints be damned!

Erika fondly remembers the time Grandma Charlotte took her and her cousins to her indoor pool. After swimming the three were instructed by Grandma to take a shower. Grandma kept going back and forth from each of their showers making sure that none of them missed a crevice that needed cleaning.

This crazy cleanliness gene moved on to Leila. Her hands are typically chaffed and dry at the end of the day, from the many times a day she washes them. She oversees the cleaning and recleaning of the dishes and silverware, before they go into the dishwasher to be recleaned. The other day the Health Inspector came into the tearoom for her annual visit. As the inspector was washing her hands and dripping on the floor, Leila kept vigilant eyes on her, wiping up her spills and handing her a towel. The inspector wanted to stick her thermometer into the batch of chicken salad Leila had just made. We didn't know where that thermometer had been, so Leila quickly put a spoon full of Chicken Salad on a plate for the inspector to inspect. I guess the inspector didn't live by the gospel "Cleanliness is next to Godliness!"

How many times is too many times to go to the bathroom? We had a table of 4 ladies that could not stop going back and forth to the bathrooms. Even when we thought they were finally leaving, and it might be safe to get back into the water, one by one they revisited the tidy bowl man. One more for the road! We're pretty sure one of them stole the extra roll of toilet paper. When Grandma Charlotte was alive she sat in the back of the tea room near the bathrooms. Her vigilance included protecting the extra rolls of toilet paper, napkins, and tissues. No one would be able to get away with anything when eagle eye fleegle was around.

Talking about cleanliness, one of our dear customers bought us a hand washing cup. We wanted to ask her if she thought we didn't have a sink. We actually have 7 sinks in the tearoom. What are the sinks for? What is a hand washing cup for? We had to look this up on the internet. In Judaism, "kosher" means clean. The hand washing cup is a vessel to wash hands and purify them before meals, before morning prayers or on special holidays. With all the times Leila washes her hands in a day, we would need several gallons of water to refill the hand washing cup and to clean and purify her hands. We think the sinks will work just fine! After all, we are not that religious!

Sheldon, Erika's father and Leila's husband who is the head of the custodial staff and dish washer to the stars did not get the OCD cleaning gene that his family lives by. When Leila was pregnant with Erika she had days she had to lie down for an afternoon nap. She went to lie down but before she did, she asked Sheldon to make her bacon which was one of her pregnancy cravings. Sheldon put the slab of bacon into a frying pan, not separating the slices. Then he put the electric stove on high. He then wanted to clean the apartment so that Leila would wake up to a clean house. He took Pledge furniture polish to the glass cabinets. Then he used Windex on the wood furniture. Leila woke up to the sound of the smoke alarm. Not only did Sheldon burn the bacon, the glass cabinets were filmed with Pledge, and the furniture was streaked with Windex. Needless to say, Leila had to reclean the house and she did not get her desired bacon. Isn't it bad luck to deprive a pregnant woman of her cravings, or is it just a superstition. Sheldon couldn't bring home the bacon, couldn't fry it up in a pan, and in turn ruined the frying pan!

Still today we rely on Sheldon to clean the dishes, the bathrooms and the floors. Leila still inspects what Sheldon tries to do and many times asks him to redo the task properly, which means, to Leila's standards! Leila does not understand if a puppy can train its parents, why can't Sheldon be trained. Maybe a scratch behind the ear would help. Treats are typically given often.

Today, most commercials on tv contain very sad content (mostly cancers and other diseases). I say enough! TV is supposed to entertain, not depress. The puppy falls asleep in the car seat in the back of the car listening to "The Wheels of the Bus" over and over again. The doggie parents feel that they have a chance to turn off the annoying song. The puppy immediately wakes up crying barking. The music goes back on. If dogs can learn good tricks, why can't Sheldon?

THINGS YOU SHOULD NOT DO IN OR IN FRONT OF THE GLASS DOORS OR WINDOWS OF A TEA ROOM

When people are no longer young, they forget our windows are an open book. We always say live and let live. We always did, we always did, we always did. But, in this ever changing world in which we live in, people give it a try. To do things on the sly, in front of our eyes, unconscious to those around them.

We don't understand why people do not realize that glass is see through. They do not realize a door is not the best place to stand. They pace back and forth in front of the door on their phones and do not seem to realize that the doors do open! Also, scratching and other habits should not be done in front of glass. We say what happens in the tearoom stays in the tearoom. But that does not include outside the tea room!

This is not what they call Window Voyeurism. These people are in front of our store windows. Are they unconscious? Do they not realize that there are people sitting at our tables having afternoon tea? They catch a glimpse of what is happening right outside the windows and then take an immediate double take.

Children were notorious for leaving their finger and nose prints on our store windows. Now there are many more seniors leaving their smudges on our freshly washed windows. We think as you age you can't see as well and by pressing against the glass they can get a bird's eye view of all we have to offer. Then there are those who cup their hands over their eyes to look in. You really need to see their faces from our side of the glass. The faces they make are hilarious.

Leila worked for a Bank that had clear glass offices. She remembers the day that an officer of the Bank, being late for an important meeting, came rushing to the office. The glass had just been cleaned. She went for the door but went face first into the glass leaving her red lipstick on the glass. She also went backwards down to the floor, since she knocked herself out!

Lesson learned. Don't do anything in front of a glass window that you would not do inside. A tea room is a special elegant domain. People are held to higher standards of behavior. Ask Emily Post for teatime etiquette!

ERIKA CONTINUES TO RULE THE ROOST

Erika would state that she is the Warden of Cell Block 8 managing everything and everyone from the beginning to the end of the day! There's no beating around the bush, Erika keeps everyone (Leila) on task and runs a tight ship. Our day begins: Erika wakes Leila up with a shout out. On her way down the stairs, Erika visits the laundry room, picking out clean clothes and undies for Leila. Public Service Announcement: Always Remember to Wear Clean Underwear, you never know if you will get hit by a bus! Then, Erika takes Leila for a quick drive through breakfast, getting Leila her egg whites in a bowl with a diet coke. As soon as they get to the tea room a list of what needs to be baked that day is handed off to Leila with a priority of which needs to be made first and so on.

Leila was busy preparing for our special Holiday High Tea. There was still much to be done and a harried Leila was kept bustling in the kitchen, trying to finish all that was set to be served. Erika was on the phone helping one customer after another with last-minute shopping needs. Sheldon comes out of the men's room to inform Erika (still on the phone) that there is a small drip of water in the bathroom.

Suddenly, we all heard a loud boom! Let's just call it the "Great Christmas Flood"! We all ran to the back of the tea room where the bathrooms are located. We saw a flood of water seeping under the doors. There was no shut off valve in the entire store and we had to call the city to get the water shut off! So as we stood in water up to our ankles, Erika the strict taskmaster told Leila to keep on task in the kitchen. "Man your Stations" she yelled.

This reminded Leila about her days in the Bank. The fire alarm went off and smoke was pouring out of the air conditioner units in the ceiling. This happened over the call center. Leila's Small Business Department was on the side wall. The head of the call center told everyone to "Man their Phones" since customers came first. She further told them that she would not let them burn. Leila came out of her department and quickly got her staff and the call center staff out of the building, as she met the Fire Department at the door.

Erika would have let Leila drown as long as customers got their scones! "Come thunder, come lightning, come flood or high water – the scones must be done!"

When it comes to making decisions on themed events and their dedicated menus Erika continues to manage it all. Leila teases Erika. She states that Erika has one brilliant thought a day! Afterward, she needs a nap. It hurts! One brilliant thought for Erika, one giant step for mankind!

Holiday Memories or The Ghost of Holidays Past Recipes

MEET ME IN ST. LOUIS

Meet Me in St. Louis is one of our favorite Holiday musicals. How can you forget Esther's iconic red velvet dress? The bond of this close knit family sitting around the table, conversing on the details of each of their days, is quite traditional for that time period. It makes us want to relive the good old days where food connects the family unit.

Have yourself a Merry Little Christmas. Let your heart be light. Next year all our troubles will be out of sight! Holiday songs, Holiday meals, and a warm and loving Family - Warms your heart - Right?

MENU:

Tootie's Fruitie Scone

Cabbage as a Cabbage Smells Soup

Corned Beef Night Dinner Sandwich

I Need Recuperating Almond Cake with a Mixed Berry Topping

This reminds Leila of all the Holiday dinners around her dining room table. The immediate family consisted of 11 people. Leila's older sister added the revolving door of boyfriends as Holiday guest number 12. Our annual Holiday pictures became a Who's That Guy in our Holiday Memories. Later on additional people were added as the children grew. First a bunch of friends, then spouses, and lastly a new generation to feed! Each Holiday had traditional food that had to be made. Leila couldn't disappoint any member of the family. It was fun seeing how favorite recipes changed over the course of the years, as well as, requests for goody bags for all to take home and enjoy!

Erika carries on the traditions by making the tea room's Holiday menus with her favorite foods. On one hand Erika wants to share these with our tea room guests. On the other hand, Erika makes sure Leila makes enough so that she can have her fill of each delectable dish!

Almond Cake with a Mixed Berry Topping Recipe

INGREDIENTS

1 stick of Unsalted Butter (melted)

1 ¾ cups of all-purpose Flour

1 ¾ teaspoons of Baking Powder

¾ teaspoon of Salt

2/3 cup of Brown Sugar

¼ cup of finely chopped almonds

Turbinado sugar for sprinkling

2 large Eggs

2 teaspoons of pure Almond Extract

2/3 cup of Milk

¼ cup of mixed dried Berries

DIRECTIONS

1. Preheat the oven to 350 degrees.

2. Line 2 muffin tins with liners.

3. In a small bowl - whisk flour, baking powder, and salt.

4. In a large bowl – beat butter and brown sugar until light and creamy. Beat in 1 egg at a time. Add almond extract.

5. Add dry ingredients and milk alternating. Don't overmix. Stir in almonds.

6. Put even amounts of the mixture into all the cupcake liners.

7. Put dried berries on the top of each cake and sprinkle with turbinado sugar.

8. Bake for 20 minutes or until a cake tester or toothpick comes out dry.

Leila's Tasteful Tips:

- Don't be afraid to change the extract in a cake recipe to change the flavor. You can change the almond extract to pure vanilla extract, pure orange extract, pure lemon extract, etc.

- Change the nuts or leave them out completely if desired.

- For the top you can change the dried fruit (dried cranberries, dried cherries, or dried blueberries) or use chocolate chips as an alternative.

IT'S A WONDERFUL LIFE

It's a Wonderful Life is another iconic Holiday movie. With a universal theme and teaching a key life lesson, George Bailey shows all the importance of self-worth, community, and the impact of one's actions on others. We can relate to having little in the Bank as George states that they have 2 bucks left, so he is still in business!

Everytime a bell rings, an Angel gets his wings. We all need an Angel looking over our shoulder. Later in the book we will share with you the way to make the perfect teacup Angel. Holidays bring out the Angels - or the Devils?

MENU:

Clarence's Mulled Wine Scone

Uncle Billy's Holiday Cheeseball Snowman with crackers

Henry Potter's Pot Pie Quiche

Mary Bailey's Hard-Boiled Egg and Caramelized Onion Croissant

Zuzu's My Little Gingersnap Cake

It is a Wonderful Life - especially during the Holidays. Leila loves to cook and she especially loves to cook her Holiday favorites. Some of her family and friends come at lunch time and stay for dinner and late night snacks. When Leila plans her meals she needs to prepare for any time during the day.

Leila remembers her Mom Charlotte cooking while her family was enjoying without her being present. Leila wanted everything to be prepared ahead of time so she could spend time with all of her guests. Even the to go orders were finished and waiting in the fridge with names of recipients clearly written on each. See, even back then, Leila ran a restaurant!

Uncle Billy's Holiday Cheeseball Snowman Recipe

INGREDIENTS

2 8-ounce blocks of cream cheese (room temperature)

1 8-ounce bag triple cheddar cheese (room temperature)

1 teaspoon ground Black Pepper

1 teaspoon Garlic Powder

1 teaspoon Onion Powder

1 Tablespoon dried Chives

11 Whole Peppercorns (Snowman eyes, mouth and buttons)

1 baby Carrot (nose)

1 8-ounce bag finely shredded mozzarella cheese

DIRECTIONS

1. In a stand mixer with a paddle attachment - combine cream cheese, triple cheddar cheese, and spices.

2. Make the mixture into the 2 cheese balls for the snowman - make one smaller for the head.

3. Wrap the cheese balls in plastic wrap and refrigerate overnight.

4. Unwrap the cheese balls. Roll each of the cheese balls into the shredded mozzarella cheese.

5. Place the smaller cheese ball on top of the larger one.

6. Cut a small pointy piece of the baby carrot for the nose.

7. Use the whole peppercorns for the eyes, 5 for the mouth, and 3 for buttons on the large cheese ball.

Leila's Tasteful Tips

- Cheese balls can be prepared for up to 3 days in the refrigerator before making the snowman.

- Serve with your favorite crackers.

- You can change the mozzarella to any other white shredded cheese if desired.

Mary Bailey's Hard–Boiled Egg and Caramelized Onion Croissant Recipe

INGREDIENTS

6 hard-boiled eggs (I use Eggland's Best hard-boiled eggs from the Dairy section)

1 large, sweet Onion (Vidalia)

2 Tablespoons Canola Oil

1 Tablespoon Mayonnaise

1 teaspoon ground Black Pepper

1 teaspoon Garlic Powder

1 teaspoon Onion Powder

1 teaspoon dried Parsley

½ teaspoon Salt

6 Croissants

DIRECTIONS

1. Peel and dice onions.
2. Add oil to a large frying pan. Add onions and caramelize. Set aside to cool.
3. Chop eggs in a food processor. Set aside.
4. Add caramelized onions to eggs and fold in.
5. Fold in spices and mayonnaise.
6. Slice croissants and fill each with egg mixture.

Leila's Tasteful Tips:

- Substitute Olive Oil for Canola Oil, if you like the flavor of olive oil better.
- Do not make the Eggs too fine when chopping them.
- Add 1 teaspoon of dried Dill if desired for a flavor booster.
- Makes great appetizers by taking your favorite crackers and putting a small amount of egg mixture on top. (Sprinkle it with dill or paprika to keep the eggs from turning color.)

THANKSGIVING - THE FORGOTTEN HOLIDAY

Thanksgiving is the "Forgotten" holiday. It is shoved between the fun-filled adventures of Halloween and the joyful merriment of Christmas. Let me tell you all the story of the Great Pumpkin Rice Krispie Treat Disaster. Leila tried this recipe three times and three ways and each time it got worse. I use the word disaster, because it came out beyond bad. Not often does this happen, but this just didn't work! This is one recipe we are leaving out of this book.

We know that pumpkin is used in many great Thanksgiving and Halloween recipes, but this was not one of them. No faux pas, just great pumpkin recipes that are tried and true, will be shared with you. Pure Pumpkin was never a big thing in our house. CeCe, our tea hostess, changed our minds with her Pumpkin obsession. As soon as September rolls around, CeCe wants Leila to try another new Pumpkin recipe. She's converted us to pumpkin lovers. Leila uses pure Pumpkin in soups, scones, and desserts creating scrumptious delights for CeCe and our customers to enjoy!

We've included Erika's favorite pumpkin recipe. It's a Pumpkin Cheesecake Pie. What's better than a cheesecake meeting a pumpkin pie? It's the best of both worlds. Also, this recipe is not overly sweet. It is just sweet enough. Just like Erika - she is sweet enough, but not always! At the end of a huge Thanksgiving dinner, you can loosen your belt, and enjoy a small treat. A meal is not a meal without dessert. We periodically set up a three tiered server and put all the courses out at one time. This typically happens when we have a special Holiday event. In most instances, guests eat the desserts first! No judgement in the tea room - just enjoy!

Mini Pumpkin Cheesecake Pie Recipe

INGREDIENTS

1 29-ounce can of pure Pumpkin

2 8-ounce containers of whipped cream cheese

½ stick unsalted Butter, melted

3 large Eggs

1 teaspoon pure Vanilla Extract

1 Tablespoon ground Cinnamon

1 cup of granulated Sugar

¼ teaspoon Salt

1 cup Heavy Cream

12 mini–Graham Cracker Pie Shells

DIRECTIONS

1. Preheat the oven to 350 degrees.
2. With an electric hand mixer, mix all ingredients.
3. Pour evenly into the graham cracker pie shells.
4. Bake for 20 to 30 minutes until set.

Leila's Tasteful Tips:

- Serve pie warm with a scoop of vanilla ice cream on top. Everything's better with a scoop of ice cream on top. Good news, if you have a cup of tea, there are no calories. (Tea room words to live by!)

- You can add ¼ cup of nuts to give the pie a crunchy texture.

- Change an equal amount of canned sweet potatoes (drained and mashed) if you do not like pumpkin.

- Use a Nut Pie Shell to make this recipe gluten free. (Leila likes to use Almond Flour.)

MAKING LEFTOVERS INTO DELICIOUS MEALS

Making leftovers into a second delicious meal can be tricky. Let's take the Holiday Meal to a new level by elevating what we can do with the leftovers. Change up boring and make it extraordinary. When you are making a Holiday Meal you typically make a main course and several side dishes. Don't be afraid to combine things you might not think of doing. You liked these dishes separately, why not together? Change it up! Let's make the perfect bite by having all the elements on the fork together.

Leila's father lived through the depression. With ration stamps his family was allotted a certain amount of food for the week. At the age of 17, he was drafted into the army and served in Germany during WWII. In the army, they ate food that was a mystery. With living through limited food resources, Leila's father would only eat certain foods as an adult. Each dish had to be on its own plate. They couldn't touch. When Leila would cook for him, her father was a quick fan. He loved the food combinations and ate all Leila prepared. He even ate leftovers that Leila made into wonderful second meals.

Whole turkey and trimmings make a delicious and traditional Holiday meal. By making individual shepherd's pies, you get the turkey, mashed potatoes, and veggies in one dish. It is definitely a crowd pleaser that everyone will love. Leila uses Ground Turkey which is less expensive, a time saver and a different option to a Whole Turkey.

We are not leftover people, but turkey and ham are foods you can repurpose and sometimes make better the next day. Fowl is Fowl and Ham is Bacon us Crazy! Most people go for sandwiches with the leftover meats. But then what do you do with the leftover sides? You can make soup or a pot pie. Why not a casserole? Casseroles are a hearty one-dish meal that everyone loves. After all, one man's casserole is another man's hungry-man-dinner!

Holiday Casseroles

Leila's casseroles - they're what's for dinner!
Comfort food at its finest! Whether you are
starting with leftovers or starting from scratch,
bring a little warmth, joy and togetherness to your
Holiday table!

Holiday Ham Leftover Casserole Recipe

INGREDIENTS

2 cups chopped leftover cooked Ham

1 16-ounce bag of Egg Noodles

1 8-ounce bag of shredded Triple Cheddar Cheese

1 cup of leftover Green Bean casserole with the crispy Onions

1 10.5-ounce can of condensed Cream of Onion Soup

1 cup Whole Milk or Heavy Cream

1 teaspoon of ground Black Pepper

1 teaspoon of Garlic Powder

1 teaspoon of Onion Powder

2 Tablespoons of unsalted Butter (melted)

DIRECTIONS

1. Preheat the oven to 375 degrees.

2. Cook noodles as directed. Drain and set aside.

3. Add the can of onion soup and milk to the noodles.

4. Add the ham, spices and cheese.

5. Fold in the leftover green bean casserole.

6. In a 9x13 inch disposable pan, spread melted butter on the bottom.

7. Add the mixture to the buttered pan and spread evenly.

8. Bake for 30 minutes or until the top is lightly browned.

Leila's Tasteful Tips

- If you did not make a green bean casserole - add 1 14.5-ounce can of cut green beans and a 6-ounce container of crispy fried onions.

- You can substitute any other leftover vegetables (cut them into bite size pieces).

- You can substitute the meat to leftover turkey or beef.

- This casserole is great with leftover meatloaf or meatballs.

- Change up the soup type or the type of cheese to make this dish different every time.

Shepherd's Pie Recipe

INGREDIENTS

1 pound Ground Turkey (93% lean)

2 tubes refrigerated Biscuits (8 count each)

1 bag steamable frozen Mixed Vegetables (12-ounce bag)

1 low sodium Beef Broth (32-ounce container)

2 Tablespoons all-purpose Flour

1 large, sweet Onion

6 large Russett Potatoes

1 stick unsalted Butter (1/2 cup)

½ Cup Heavy Cream

1 package shredded Triple Cheddar Cheese (8-ounce package)

1 Teaspoon Kosher Salt

1 Tablespoon of each – ground black pepper, garlic powder, and onion powder

2 Tablespoons Canola Oil

DIRECTIONS

1. Preheat the oven to 375 degrees.
2. Fill 16 muffin tin spaces with cupcake papers. Set aside to assemble our 16 individual shepherd's pies.
3. Peel and dice onion.
4. Peel and quarter potatoes.
5. In a 5-quart pot place potatoes and kosher salt. Cover with water and bring to a boil. Lower heat and simmer for 10 – 12 minutes. Use a fork to see if potatoes are tender.
6. Pour out water. Using a potato masher or fork, mash the potatoes. Add the heavy cream, cheese

and butter. Add 2 teaspoons of each – ground black pepper, garlic powder, and onion powder. Set aside to cool.

7. In a large frying pan, add oil and onions. Caramelize onion until golden brown. Place in a bowl for later use.

8. In the same pan add ground turkey and cook until the meat is totally browned. Put browned meat in another bowl. When cool, crumble the meat.

9. In the same pan pour the beef broth. On medium heat, whisk in flour and the remaining 2 teaspoons of spices.

10. Open one of the biscuit tubes. Leave the second in the refrigerator until you complete the first one.

11. Between two pieces of parchment paper, place a whole biscuit.

12. Using a rolling pin. Flatten the biscuit and place in a lined muffin tin.

13. Layer meat, onions, vegetables, 2 teaspoons of the sauce until ¾ filled. Add a layer of mashed potatoes to fill the cup.

14. Bake for 20 to 25 minutes until the potatoes are lightly browned.

Leila's Tasteful Tips:

- Substitute equal amounts of ground beef or ground lamb for the ground turkey. Use leftover turkey shredded so nothing goes to waste.
- Substitute frozen steamable broccoli or any other favorite vegetable for mixed veggies.
- This will also work nicely with leftover vegetables, like green bean casserole.

Holiday Soups

Mmm Mmm good, Mmm Mmm good! Leila's Holiday soups are Mmm Mmm good! Our Holiday Soups are rich, hearty and packed with flavor. They are sooo yummy for your tummy!

WHAT MAKES A SOUP A HOLIDAY SOUP?

Did you hear about the tea room that didn't have any soup? It ran out of stock. Soup warms the soul. Everyone has a favorite soup. One thing Leila loves to add to her soups is love. The holiday season is the perfect time to create comforting, hearty meals that bring warmth and joy to the table. A festive dinner or a cozy evening with family is enhanced by a bowl of soup. From creamy bisques to ingredient-filled broths, holiday soups offer a variety of flavors that can complement any dish and satisfy every palate.

In our tea room, a meal is not complete without a perfect bowl of soup. Whichever soup is served, our guests proclaim that the soup in front of them is their favorite. This changes daily. By the way, we still ask guests if they would like a refill on the soup that they finish in minutes. We continue our "Need to Feed" efforts ensuring no one leaves the tea room hungry.

A gentleman came in to buy 4 pumpkin mugs. He was telling us story after story about his business and his friends. We don't know how it happened but we got on the subject of soup. He declared that soup was his favorite thing to eat. He said he would prefer a big bowl of home made soup to any other Holiday dish. Just talking to him for a few minutes gave us a warm feeling. We concluded that a Holiday Soup was an integral part of any Holiday meal!

To get Erika to eat vegetables at a very young age, soup became a vessel to camouflage the vegetables Leila was trying to get her to eat. To see Erika now, you would never guess that she was such a picky eater as a child. Leila learned early to hide meats and vegetables in a soup (usually chicken broth) to get Erika to eat them.

Erika had this one date that brought her home to meet the parents. His mother made chicken soup with one carrot and one piece of onion in it. Erika was wondering if there was some kind of famine that caused a shortage of these vegetables that she loved. Erika was used to Leila's chicken soup that had multiple carrots, celery pieces, onions, turnips and parsnips. Nips were Erika's favorite.

When it comes to Holiday soups there are so many to choose from. One of Leila's favorite soups to make is a Cream of Mushroom soup. By adding a tablespoon of caramelized onions and mushrooms to the creamy soup, the taste is elevated to a new level.

Another soup that Leila loves to share is a Thanksgiving Soup. It is a traditional way to use leftover turkey in a belly-warming way. Turkey is so versatile. Whenever you have turkey leftovers, there are so many ways to use them. Turkey is a great foundation for a rich and hearty soup. Add your favorite vegetables and rice to make it complete. This "Everything but the Kitchen Sink" soup uses a wide range of ingredients and appeals to all guests looking for a meal in a bowl!

A funny thing happened on the way to Publix the other day. The Turkey Factory burned down! Don't worry - no turkeys were hurt in the fire. The problem was that there were no turkey loins for Leila this week! Boo hoo. . .

Mushroom and Caramelized Onion Soup Recipe

INGREDIENTS

3 12-ounce bags frozen mushrooms

1 12-ounce container of baby Portobello Mushrooms

1 large, sweet Onion (Vidalia)

1 32-ounce container of low-sodium Chicken Stock

½ cup Heavy Cream

2 Tablespoons of Canola Oil

2 teaspoons of ground Black Pepper

2 teaspoons of Garlic Powder

2 teaspoons of Onion Powder

1 Tablespoon dried Parsley

DIRECTIONS

1. Peel and dice onion. Wash and dice fresh mushrooms.

2. In a large frying pan put in canola oil. Put on medium for a few minutes until the oil heats up. Then put in diced onions.

3. Stir onions occasionally until browned. Don't over stir or else the onions will not brown.

4. Add the diced fresh mushrooms. Fry until the mushrooms are soft.

5. In a 5-quart stock pot put stock, the 3 bags of frozen mushrooms, and spices and bring to a boil.

6. Using an immersion blender, puree the soup until smooth.

7. Add Heavy Cream. Add caramelized onions and mushrooms to garnish.

Leila's Tasteful Tips:

- If you want just the creamy soup without the caramelized onions and mushrooms, leave off the fresh onion and mushrooms.

- Add ½ cup of cooked barley or rice to add more texture to the creamy soup.

Thanksgiving Soup Recipe

INGREDIENTS

1 24-ounce boneless Turkey Loin

2 steamable 12-ounce bags of frozen mixed vegetables (Broccoli, Cauliflower, and Carrots)

2 microwavable pouches of Long Grain and Wild Rice

2 teaspoons of ground Black Pepper

2 teaspoons of Garlic Powder

2 teaspoons of Onion Powder

1 Tablespoon dried Parsley

3 32-ounce containers of low sodium chicken broth

½ cup Heavy Cream

DIRECTIONS

1. In a 5-quart stock pot, cook the turkey loin in 1 of the containers of chicken stock for an hour or until the turkey is soft. (If a fork goes in easily then it is thoroughly cooked.)
2. Let the turkey cool and cut into small chunks.
3. Microwave the rice pouches for 90 seconds.
4. Microwave the mixed vegetables. When cool, cut into pieces.
5. In a large stock pot, put stock, turkey, rice and vegetables. (Make sure rice is separated.)
6. Add spices and bring to a boil. Add heavy cream.

Leila's Tasteful Tips:

- You can cook the turkey loin in advance to save time.
- Substitute chicken or another meat for the turkey loin.
- Leave meat out of the soup to make it vegetarian.

OUR WICKEDLY GOOD HOLIDAY EVENT

When Erika suggested a "Wickedly" good Holiday soup, Leila jumped at the chance to make something green. Leila immediately thought of all types of green soups. A chilled avocado soup came to mind. A mixture of avocado and cucumber makes a great tasting soup. Soup, whether hot or cold, is comforting and versatile, making it a perfect choice for a Holiday meal.

Making a color coordinated meal makes a wonderful Holiday setting. Whether you are creating a themed event or just a family Holiday get together, making everything match is fun and tasty.

THE WICKED "GREEN AND PINK" MENU

Pink goes good with Green Strawberry Pistachio Scone

Elphaba's Chilled Avocado Soup

Popular "It's our most Popular" Chicken Salad Croissant

Dill Cucumber Sandwitch

Nessa's "I'm not Green with Envy" Bacon and Spinach Quiche

Together We're Unlimited Key Lime Panna Cotta and a Strawberry Shortcake Cupcake

Cold Avocado Soup Recipe

INGREDIENTS

2 English Cucumbers

1 bag of frozen chopped Onions

2 8-ounce containers of Mild Guacamole

1 16-ounce container of Sour Cream

1 32-ounce container of Heavy Cream

2 teaspoons of ground Black Pepper

2 teaspoons of Garlic Powder

2 teaspoons of Onion Powder

¼ cup sliced fresh Scallions

DIRECTIONS

1. Peel and cube the cucumbers.

2. In a stock pot put the stock and the cucumbers. Bring to a boil and then lower the heat to simmer.

3. Add the spices.

4. Simmer until the cucumbers are fork tender, approximately 15 minutes.

5. Using an immersion blender, cream the soup and the cucumbers.

6. Cool the soup in the refrigerator.

7. When cool, add the sour cream, the guacamole and the heavy cream with either the immersion blender or an electric hand mixer until fully blended.

8. Put soup in the refrigerator overnight. Top with sliced scallions. Serve cold.

Leila's Tasteful Tips:

- Pipe a dollop of sour cream as a garnish.
- Take a fresh avocado and cut into thin slices. Garnish the soup with the fresh avocado to add texture.
- Take a fresh lime or fresh lime zest for garnish and a little acid added to the taste.

HAPPY HOLIDAY TEA SANDWICHES

You've heard of the Sandwich King, we are the Sandwich Queens! Girl Scout Cookies are made with real girl scouts and our Finger Tea Sandwiches are made with real fingers. You can always make the typical tea sandwiches, but we make them with panache. Put the sass and class back into the world of tea room finger sandwiches.

Our tea sandwiches are so good, they are like a "hug" for your taste buds! Use the real thing baby when making the best sandwiches and add a bit of flair. We only use real chicken or turkey, tuna, mayo, butter, etc. as our ingredients. We have not changed from the day we started our business. We use the finest ingredients to get the best results.

Our Holiday tea sandwiches include a Turkey, Cranberry and Brie sandwich and an Italian Tuna Salad sandwich. These colorful sandwiches remind folks that they eat first with their eyes. These sandwiches are love at first sight. They are full of wonderful ingredients that add great flavor that would even satisfy the "Earl of Sandwich".

Why did the Turkey, Cranberry and Brie Sandwich break up with the baguette? It found someone with more "panache".

What's the Italian Tuna Salad Sandwich's favorite game? Tuna-ment!

Turkey, Cranberry and Brie Sandwich Recipe

INGREDIENTS

1 1.5-pound boneless Turkey Loin

1 32-ounce container of low-sodium Chicken Stock

1 14-ounce can of whole berry Cranberry Sauce

¼ cup of Mayonnaise

1 teaspoon of ground Black Pepper

1 teaspoon of Garlic Powder

1 teaspoon of Onion Powder

1 4-ounce chunk of Brie Cheese

1 16-ounce package seeded Jewish Rye Bread (Seedless is fine, too!)

DIRECTIONS

1. In a medium stock pot, bring the turkey loin to boil in the chicken stock. Then, lower the heat and simmer until turkey is cooked through, 45-60 minutes. Test the doneness by putting a fork in the thickest part of the loin. If it goes into the meat easily, then it is done.

2. Set aside to cool. Using a serrated knife cut the cooked turkey loin into ⅛ to ¼ inch thick slices.

3. Toast the rye bread (2 pieces per person). Cut off the edges and shape into triangles.

4. In a small bowl, mix the mayonnaise with the spices. Smear each of the slices of bread with the mayonnaise.

5. Cut the Brie into ⅛ to ¼ inch thick slices.

6. Place 1-2 slices of turkey on the bottom slice of bread. Put a slice of Brie on top.

7. Spread a teaspoon of the Cranberry Sauce. (Not too much or else the bread will get wet.)

8. Top with the Rye Bread.

Leila's Tasteful Tips:

- You can use jellied Cranberry Sauce if you do not like the Whole Berry.
- You can change the bread choice as you like it.
- You can use leftover turkey or chicken to make this sandwich.

Italian Tuna Salad Sandwich Recipe

INGREDIENTS

2 cans of chunk light Tuna in Olive Oil

¼ cup of diced Roasted Red Peppers

¼ cup of diced Red Onions

1 stalk of Celery washed and diced

1 Tablespoon of fresh Lemon Juice

1 Tablespoon glazed Lemon Peel

1 Tablespoon dried Parsley

1 teaspoon of ground Black Pepper

1 teaspoon of Garlic Powder

1 teaspoon of Onion Powder

DIRECTIONS

1. Open the cans of tuna and put the tuna into a large bowl. Using a fork, flake the tuna.
2. Dice the peppers and put in the bowl with the tuna.
3. Dice the celery and add.
4. Dice the onions and add.
5. Add the spices, lemon juice and lemon peel.
6. Mix all the ingredients.

Leila's Tasteful Tips:

- If the tuna salad is too dry, add a ½ - 1 Tablespoon of olive oil.
- Instead of the roasted red peppers, you can use a fresh red sweet pepper.
- Additional items you can add: Kalamata Olives diced, Capers, or diced Tomatoes.
- Lettuce cups are the new sandwich! They are the carb-friendly alternative to bread.

Poached Pear Chicken Salad in Flower Cups Recipe

CHICKEN SALAD INGREDIENTS

1-pound boneless skinless Chicken Breast Cutlets

32-ounce low-sodium Chicken Stock

¼ cup of chopped dried Pears

½ of a 10-12 ounce jar of Pear Preserves

¼ cup of Mayonnaise

2 teaspoons of ground Black Pepper

2 teaspoons of Garlic Powder

2 teaspoons of Onion Powder

DIRECTIONS

1. In a medium stock pot, put chicken stock and chicken cutlets. Bring to boil, lower heat, and simmer for 30 to 40 minutes until fork tender.

2. Drain and let the chicken cool. (You can prepare the chicken the night before.)

3. In a food processor coarsely grind the chicken.

4. Add the mayonnaise and pear preserves.

5. Add the spices and the dried pears.

6. Using a round cookie scoop, put a scoop of chicken salad into the flower cups to serve.

Leila's Tasteful Tips

- Chicken can be chunked or pulled if larger pieces are desired.
- You can use canned pears chopped into bite size pieces instead of dried pears.
- Substitute peach preserves and dried peaches (or drained diced peaches in a can) for a more summery taste.

FLOWER CUP INGREDIENTS

1 package of your favorite Bread (Leila uses 12 grain)

3 inch flower shaped Cookie Cutter

2 regular-size Muffin/Cupcake Pans

2 Tablespoons of Butter (melted)

DIRECTIONS

1. Preheat the oven to 350 degrees.
2. Take a slice of the bread. Using a rolling pin, roll over the slice of bread to flatten it out.
3. Using a flower cookie cutter, cut out the flower shape.
4. In the dry muffin/cupcake pan, push the bread sheet in the center, flattening it up the sides.
5. Brush with the melted butter.
6. Bake for 7 minutes until lightly browned.
7. Cool.

Leila's Tasteful Tips:

- Can use a flavored bread such as Cinnamon Swirl.
- You can make the flower bread bowls in advance and store them in a covered plastic container. They last for up to a week on the counter.
- You can use a different shaped cookie cutter to go with the Holiday.

INSPIRATION COMES FROM EVERYWHERE WE GO

Leila and Erika look for inspiration to create unique flavors of tea sandwiches wherever their travels take them. When we went to Arizona a few weeks ago, we tried an appetizer of Fig and Ricotta Toast. As Leila chewed each tasty bite, Leila contemplated how she could enhance this already good treat. Leila thought by adding crushed pistachios and diced dried figs on the top of the ricotta that would be great. Additionally, Erika asked her to add a drizzle of honey. Wala! Success!

Two ladies called for a reservation for Afternoon Tea. After asking about the menu of the day, the two asked for 3 sliced ham sandwiches instead - no mayo, no mustard, just sad, dry lonely ham. They forfeited the Holiday Poached Pear Chicken Salad Cups, the Holiday Ham Salad Sandwich and the Quiche Lorraine for 3 dry deli Ham sandwiches. How absurd! Leila needed to keep her culinary skills intact, so Leila decided to take the basic sandwich and add her favorite Holiday touches.

She quickly decided to make some more special Holiday tea sandwiches. Leila used fresh pears, dried pears and canned pears to add an uplifting flavor to her Holiday Chicken Salad. Then, fruits such as pineapple and glazed cherries enhanced a good diced honey Ham. These sweet and savory delights make Holiday lunches extremely special.

Embrace the Holiday Season by making the perfect Holiday Sandwich that uses the best festive flavors! Don't be afraid to try incorporating your favorite dried or fresh fruits, nuts, berries and spices. Why have a dud spud when you can have a greater potater!

Holiday Ham Salad Recipe

INGREDIENTS

1-pound chunk of Honey Ham from the deli counter

2 Tablespoons of Honey Dijon Mustard

¼ cup of Mayonnaise

2 teaspoons of ground Black Pepper

2 teaspoons of Garlic Powder

2 teaspoons of Onion Powder

2 teaspoons of dried Chives

1 3-ounce can of Pineapple Tidbits (drained)

2 Tablespoons of dried Glazed Cherries (chopped)

DIRECTIONS

1. In the food processor, grind the honey ham.
2. In a large bowl, put ground ham and add the mustard and mayonnaise.
3. Add all of the spices.
4. Add the pineapple and cherries.
5. Serve on a Hawaiian Roll or your favorite bread.

Leila's Tasteful Tips:

- You can use leftover ham from your Holiday dinner.
- You can substitute fresh parsley or scallions for the dried chives.
- You can use a jar of apricot preserves and dried apricots instead of the pineapple and cherries.

Fig and Ricotta Toast with Pistachio Nuts Recipe

INGREDIENTS

4 thick slices of Sourdough Bread

¼ cup Ricotta Cheese

¼ cup Fig Preserves

¼ cup chopped Pistachios

¼ cup of dried chopped Figs

¼ cup Orange Blossom Honey

DIRECTIONS

1. Preheat the oven to 400 degrees.

2. Toast the slices of bread on a covered cookie sheet.

3. Toast for 10 minutes or until the bread is lightly browned.

4. Then add a thin smear of the fig preserves on each.

5. Put a thin smear of ricotta cheese on the bread.

6. Top the bread with the chopped pistachios and the chopped figs.

7. Drizzle the tops of each bread slice with the honey.

Leila's Tasteful Tips:

- You can change the preserves to any flavor you like.
- You can use compatible flavors of honey other than orange blossom.

HANUKKAH HOLIDAY TEA SANDWICHES

We can't forget our favorite Hanukkah tea sandwiches. There's nothing like a smear of chopped liver on a little Challah roll. One man's Pate is another man's Chopped Liver. All we know is that if you make it right it is dee-lic-ious! We just got back from a vacation in Arizona. We found a chain of New York Delis that serve chopped liver on small challah rolls. We didn't know that chopped liver could be so sour. It was bad, bad, bad and the roll was super stale! They need to try our chopped liver. . . Our Bubbie would turn over in her grave if anyone thought that this chopped liver was edible chopped liver.

The best part of Hanukkah is making a potted Brisket. This tender beef recipe makes the best sandwich ever. Slice it thick or thin for your favorite lunch or dinner meal. Add some potatoes to make it a stew.

What did the Brisket Sandwich say to the French Toast? You're too sweet; I need some Meat in my life!

Sorry Pate, they took all the food in the fridge and went on a vegetarian picnic. What am I chopped liver?

Why do Superheroes love Erika's Tea Room Holiday Tea Sandwiches? Because they're always "Super Delicious"!

All kidding aside, stop spinning your dreidel or counting your chocolate gelt; just savor the best Hanukkah Tea Sandwiches. It is not Hanukkah without them!

Hanukkah Chopped Liver on a Challah Roll Recipe

INGREDIENTS

1-pound fresh Chicken Livers (Wash and put in a colander.)

2 hard-boiled Eggs (I use Eggland's Best hard-boiled eggs by the fresh eggs)

1 medium sweet Onion (chopped finely)

2 Tablespoons Canola Oil

1 teaspoon of ground Black Pepper

1 teaspoon of Garlic Powder

1 teaspoon of Onion Powder

1 teaspoon of table Salt

DIRECTIONS

1. In a large frying pan, add oil to coat bottom and add chopped onions.

2. Caramelize onions until lightly browned.

3. Add chicken livers and spices to the onions.

4. Brown each piece of liver until completely cooked through.

5. Chop livers in a food processor and set aside to cool.

6. Coarse chop hard-boiled eggs, also in the food processor.

7. Fold eggs into liver and taste to see if additional spices are needed (Add ½ teaspoon of the above spices as needed.)

8. Refrigerate for at least a few hours to cool or overnight.

9. When ready to serve, cut the roll in half. Put a nice amount of chopped liver on the roll and enjoy.

Leila's Tasteful Tips:

- You can add a slice of your favorite lettuce on the top of the sandwich.
- Add a good Kosher Pickle on the side of the sandwich for a great Hanukkah treat.
- Enjoy with crackers for a late evening snack.

Hanukkah Brisket Sandwich Recipe

INGREDIENTS

1 4-5 pound fresh Brisket (trimmed of most of the fat, lean)

1 cup Water

1 cup of Heinz Ketchup

2 teaspoons of ground Black Pepper

2 teaspoons of Garlic Powder

2 teaspoons of Onion Powder

2 teaspoons of ground Paprika

1 12-ounce bag frozen diced Onions

1 12-ounce bag frozen sliced Carrots

6 small Dinner Rolls

DIRECTIONS

1. In a large stockpot put all the ingredients and bring to a boil. Reduce heat and simmer covered for 2 ½ to 3 hours or until meat is tender.

2. Half way through the cooking process, turn the meat over. Add ½ cup or more of water if needed. (This will prevent the meat from sticking to the pot.)

3. When the meat is soft, remove the meat from the pot and let it rest before cutting it into thin slices. (You can cool the meat in the refrigerator for a few hours or overnight before slicing it.)

4. Use an immersion blender to puree the vegetables for a gravy for the sandwich.

5. Pile the meat on the roll and add some gravy. Enjoy!

Leila's Tasteful Tips:

- If serving the brisket for dinner, do not puree the vegetables.
- Add 2 cans of whole potatoes to the pot. This makes the brisket into a wonderful stew.
- You can also add 2 stalks of celery. (washed and cut into ½ inch slices)
- You can use Hawaiian rolls or slider rolls if you prefer.

TEATIME HOLIDAY SONGS AND MORE!

Music is a huge part of our family. We take great joy in theater and musical movies. Holidays in our house always included someone playing piano and the rest of us singing along. There is no time era of song that we did not honor. We loved the old musicals such as Deanna Durbin, Billie Holiday, Rodgers and Hammerstein, Rocky Horror, and even today with Wicked. The Shanoff family has a very theatrical demeanor.

Long trips were less tedious with continued singing of all our favorite tunes. When the Shanoff family travelled, name that tune and themed sing-a-longs were an expected activity. Leila got this from her upbringing. When her father took them on their long car trips either up to the Catskills or to Niagara Falls, Canada the gang sang all of Dad's favorites.

Even when we did not know the exact words to a song – our motto of just sing loud, sing proud, and sing off key gets us singing. This was ever so evident when Grandma Charlotte went into her rendition of What's It All About Alfie or Two Floors Down They're Having a Party. Charlotte was in the chorus in school, they told her she could not carry a tune, but in those days, they never left anyone out. They should have told her to lip sync. She hit notes only dogs could hear and then they would turn around and run!

Another favorite pastime is taking any song and changing the words. Leila started rewriting songs in High School when she had Sing. This was a competition between teams. Just like in Pitch Perfect where they competed with song mash-ups, Sing was where the different grades (Seniors, Juniors, and Sophomores) rewrote songs and sung them to a group of judges and the entire school.

Today, Leila and Erika take songs and rewrite the words to go along with their themed events and murder mysteries. Give us a theme and we'll sing you a song. We will try not to sing out of key. We'll get by with a little help from our friends.

Holidays are the best time to rewrite festive Holiday tunes with our own flair! Everyone must sing for their dinner! In your house does caroling come before or after dinner? When people come to our Murder Mysteries, they find clues in the rewritten songs. This helps them solve the murder mystery and find out "Who Dun It"!

Our Holiday Murder Mystery helps Santa find the missing Rudolph. There might not be a Christmas if Rudolph can't guide Santa's sleigh. After all we are in Florida, there is no snow - we need Rudolph!

SANTA BABY

Santa Baby
Put a tea set under the tree
For me
I'm a tea drinking girl
You see
So hurry down my chimney tonight

Santa Cutie
Fill my stocking up with scones
And jam
Add a little honey oh yes
You can
And hurry down my chimney tonight

Santa Honey
One thing I really must have
Real bad
Having tea time with you
I'm glad
And hurry down my chimney tonight!

ALVIN AND THE CHIPMUNKS – CHRISTMAS DON'T BE LATE

Christmas, Christmas time is near
Time for scones that make you cheer
We've been good for goodness sake
So hurry, Christmas off we bake!

Want a tea set, yes we do
If we don't get it, boo hoo hoo!
We can hardly, stand the wait
Please Christmas, don't be late!

THE 8 DAYS OF HANUKKAH

On the first day of Hanukkah, my true love gave to me
A bagel with a cream cheese smear

On the second day of Hanukkah, my true love gave to me
Two spinning dreidels, and a bagel with a cream cheese smear

On the third day of Hanukkah, my true love gave to me
Three matzah balls, two spinning dreidels and a bagel with a cream cheese smear

On the fourth day of Hanukkah, my true love gave to me

Four jelly donuts, three matzah balls, two spinning dreidels and a bagel with a cream cheese smear

On the fifth day of Hanukkah, my true love gave to me
Five golden latkes, four jelly donuts, three matzah balls, two spinning dreidels and a bagel with a cream cheese smear

On the sixth day of Hanukkah, my true love gave to me
Six chocolate gelt, five golden latkes, four jelly donuts, three matzah balls, two spinning dreidels and a bagel with a cream cheese smear

On the seventh day of Hanukkah, my true love gave to me
Seven lighted candles, six chocolate gelt, five golden latkes, four jelly donuts, three matzah balls, two spinning dreidels and a bagel with a cream cheese smear

On the eighth day of Hanukkah, my true love gave to me
Eight wrapped gifts, seven lighted candles, six chocolate gelt, five golden latkes, four jelly donuts, three matzah balls, two spinning dreidels and a bagel with a cream cheese smear

TEATIME TRIVIA

1) What did Mrs. Claus tell the stressed-out Santa?
   Santa relax - enjoy the Holiday Festiva-teas!

2) What is Santa's favorite teatime song?
   Oh, Christmas tea, Oh Christmas tea! How tasty are your tea leaves!

3) Who is Santa's best teatime friend?
   Frost-tea the Snowman

4) What is Rudolph's teatime Holiday wish?
   Wishing you all a Beau-tea-ful Holiday Season!

5) I'm on a Tea diet this Christmas.
   It's all about Steeping my way to Joy!

6) What's Santa's favorite type of Tea?
   A Jolly Good Brew!

7) Why did the Teapot file a Police Report?
   It got mugged at the Holiday Party!

8) What do you call a Festive Tea that Sings?
   A Merry Infusician!

9) Why did the Christmas Tea break up with the Coffee?
    It found someone who was more Brew-tea-ful!

10) My Christmas Tea is sooo good it should be on the Nice List!

NAME THAT TEA SET

Just like we change the name to songs, we love to name that tea set. Sometimes it is as simple as using the flower or picture on it, but mostly it works with the season or a fun play on words. Our Holiday tea sets range from playful to traditional and everything in between. We like to claim that we have something for everybody's taste and preferences. We go back to not leaving any tea set left unbought or leaving any lonely tea set left alone on the shelf, but in the words of Buzz Lightyear "To Infinity and Beyond", no tea sets left behind!

Our tea set names are inspired by famous movie stars such as our Holly Berry set or sometimes more whimsical such as our Santa's Sleighride, Rudolph's Retreat, or Peter Pumpkin Patch tea sets. We love traditional tea sets and name them appropriately such as our Christmas Rose tea set and adding a dramatic feel we named our Monet's Sunflowers in Bloom.

We have Cardinals and Snowmen, and Nutcracker tea sets. Santa and Gingerbread cookie jars with them. But do you recall, our most famous tea sets of all! Erika named a tea set with a very classical name. It was shaped like a Penguin. You might call it the same! All of the other Penguins weren't as cute as he! So Erika called him Precious and everyone shouted with glee!

NO HOLIDAY TEA SET LEFT BEHIND

It was just another day at Erika's Tea Room. The tearoom was a mess, white dots of foam spewed on the light slate tiles that made up the typically clean floors. Large holiday orders arrived and needed to be checked for damages, leaving the place less than pristine. Erika knew that her mother Leila would not be happy seeing the tea room as is. There were only 40 more boxes that needed to be opened, inspected and then carted off to one of the eight storage units. All this had to be completed before the usual afternoon downpour. Another rainy day in Clermont, Florida – how common! People can move quickly between raindrops, but oversized packing boxes can not move that fast, especially with Sheldon's typical slow-mo actions. Since everyone was in their place, it seemed that the day was normal.

Just as we cleaned up the 40 boxes of tea sets, the UPS truck pulled up in front of the store. Wonderful, another 20 boxes of tea sets to check in. As Leila and Erika shop for their newest tea sets, their favorite song instinctually seeps out of their mouths. This song is sung to the tune "I Hope I Get it" from a "Chorus Line". These are the words.

> God we hope we get it, We hope we get it
> How many Teapots do we Need, We need to get them
> Such an Expression, How many Plates did we Receive
> We really need this Set, Or we'll be quite Upset
> We really need this Set

So we are off to do more Holiday shopping for the store. Ready, Set, Go - do not leave any tea set left unbought! Don't forget all the additional Holiday buyables that would team well with Holiday flavors of scones.

HOLIDAY GIFTING – GIFTS YOU CAN'T RETURN OR REGIFT

Let's start by saying that Holidays are always exciting and special. Erika assists each customer in finding the perfect Holiday gifts. After all, Holidays are all about the gifts. Leila would say that they are all about the food. Gifts – Food – It is definitely a toss up!

Last minute shopping – Bah Humbug! It didn't work out well for Scrooge. True shoppers know to start their Holiday shopping at least 6 months prior to the Holiday. Everyone knows that you find the best Holiday gifts when it is 100 degrees outside. Die hard gifters start their Holiday shopping on December 26th and continue throughout the year.

You can imagine what type of shoppers we are. If shopping was an Olympic sport, we'd be gold medalists. After all the full 8 storage units, full house of boxes, and full shelves in the store are evidence of what we preach. When customers tell us they have no more room for one more tea set – Erika replies there is always room for Jello and of course one more Tea Set!

After helping a customer for an hour and having several tea sets side by side for the customer to compare, Erika asked the customer if there might be a specific style tea set she might be looking for. The customer replied, "When the tea set jumps out at her she will know it's the one!" Erika retorted, "I've seen a lot of things that jump out, but never a tea set!" She was not too sure that our tea sets were trained to do tricks such as jumping out! We have thousands of tea sets (literally) but not one of them jumped. Maybe, if we ask our manufacturers nicely they could create jumping tea sets!

At age six, Leila knew that Erika was the cutest little girl on the planet! There was nothing she wouldn't do for her, buy for her, begrudge her. Erika called her into the den and showed Leila a brand-new talking Cabbage Patch doll on a tv advertisement. "Mom I need one", she squealed. Leila found out that on Black Friday Bradley's Department Store would be selling 100 of these dolls. They would be opening at 6 AM. Leila and her sister Gail arrived at Bradley's around midnight with their folding chairs. The line was already forming. They needed to be the first to get their hands on their daughters' requested gifts. So they sat on the line, took turns cat napping and waiting for the 6 AM wake up call. At 6 AM on the dot, the door opened, the crowds rushed in, their feet did not reach the floor, as the crowds carried them into the store. Each of us grabbed a doll. Leila grabbed one that was blue eyed and blonde haired, as Gail grabbed a redhead with green eyes.

The funny part of the story is: when Erika went to play with her new doll and it began to talk, the doll grabbed hold of Erika's hair. From that moment on, Erika was terrified and refused to play with it! She actually cried when she saw it. The doll was placed back in its box and put in the dolly graveyard at the bottom of Erika's closet, not to be heard of again. Leila should have waited for the doll to jump out and since it didn't she should have left it on the shelf!

Erika wanted a dog from the time she was little, but Leila worked long hours and knew she would have to be the dog's caregiver. Not having enough time, but wanting to make Erika happy, Leila bought Penelope Pitstop. Erika loved her small dog that did not need to be walked and only needed to be watered or fed once a day. She petted her beige furred dog, but grew weary that it did not bark. She kept asking Leila why her dog didn't bark. Leila explained that young dogs didn't bark. Gullably, Erika bought the deception. After a while, Leila told Erika that Penelope Pitstop was really a long-haired guinea pig. Erika never asked for a dog again! Soon after, Erika grew tired of her pet and did not miss her when Leila brought Penelope to the shelter.

When Leila was 5, her parents allowed her to bring home a little white puppy. A box of abandoned puppies was left outside the bungalow the family stayed at in the summers in the Catskill Mountains. Leila promised to take care of the puppy and love the puppy to the moon and back again. Being so cute, her mother could not refuse. See leaf (Erika) doesn't fall far from the tree (Leila). Leila loved the puppy so much that she kept hugging the puppy tightly. The puppy grew tired of these hugs and decided to give Leila a warning bite. The bite drew blood, so the puppy was taken to the shelter and given a better home out of Leila's voracious grip!

Regifting is another oxi-moron! Is it a gift or a regift – only the gifter knows the truth. If you didn't like the gift why do you expect someone else might! Each summer Leila would start her Holiday shopping diligently looking for 8 gifts for her 2 nieces and nephew. Leila searched high and low to choose the perfect gifts for her special family. Then Erika's Aunts gave her their present. One Aunt gave her a pair of pajamas that was ten times too big for her scented with her Aunt's perfume. REGIFT personified. Then the second Aunt gave Erika a plaid poncho, one of her agents bought her that she didn't care for. It looked like a horse blanket. Again REGIFT – if you didn't like the horse blanket, why would you think I would like it!

The best part about gifting or regifting is that no one has ever regifted our scones. They have only reluctantly shared them. After all, what is better than one scone – a box of scones!

HOLIDAY SCONES

It's the most wonderful time of the year for Holiday Scones. It is also the most wonderful time of year for chocolate. Shipping chocolate scones can be most challenging in 100 degree weather, so Holiday Time is Chocolate Time - Yippie!

Scones deserve more attention during the Holiday season. Our scones are the perfect Holiday treat to compliment your favorite cup of tea. Combining chocolate with nuts, fruits, cookie pieces, spices and candy makes a mouthful of deliciousness.

We set aside all the chocolates from all over the world and bring them out to create holiday combinations such as chocolate strawberry or german chocolate cake. We also use the best dried fruits that are more prevalent during the Holiday time. Figs and dates combined with cinnamon, vanilla, caramel and butterscotch are a few of our delectable Holiday ideas. Pecans, walnuts, and almonds are used annually, but hazel nuts and pine nuts elevate our Holiday scone flavors.

We have chosen two of our favorite Holiday Scones combinations. These are easy to make and make a great gift for yourself, family and friends. Date Nut Buttermilk Scones and Chocolate Eggnog Scones.

Date Nut Buttermilk Scones offer a sweet and nutty flavor. Perfect for afternoon tea or as a quick snack, these scones are light, fluffy, and packed with the rich taste of dates and crunchy walnuts. The tangy taste of the buttermilk balances the sweetness creating a harmonious flavor profile.

The Chocolate Eggnog Scones have rich egginess, sweet vanilla, a splash of nutmeg and cinnamon and semi sweet chocolate chips. These scones are perfect for Christmas morning. What's better than the warm smells of cinnamon and nutmeg!

There are just a few reasons that Erika deems it necessary for entering her mother's domain, "The Kitchen".

1. To take a picture or video
2. To get a sample. "Quality Control"
3. To check on what Leila is doing, "Time Management"
If not, one of the above, Erika cannot find the kitchen!

Date Nut Buttermilk Scones Recipe

INGREDIENTS

3 cups of all-purpose Flour

1 Tablespoon of Flour to roll out dough

1/3 cup of granulated Sugar

1 teaspoon Salt

2 ½ teaspoons Baking Powder

½ teaspoon Baking Soda

¾ cup (1 ½ sticks) of cold Unsalted Butter

1 cup of Buttermilk

¼ cup of pitted chopped Dates

¼ cup of chopped Walnuts

DIRECTIONS

1. Preheat the oven to 350 degrees.
2. Line cookie sheet with Parchment Paper. Cut another sheet of Parchment Paper to roll out dough.
3. Using a pastry blender: Combine the flour, sugar, salt, baking powder, and baking soda in a large bowl.
4. Using the pastry blender: Add butter to dry ingredients forming a coarse meal.
5. Using the pastry blender: Add buttermilk and mix until combined.
6. Add dates and nuts.
7. Using your hands knead the dough and form 2 balls.
8. Flour Parchment Paper, roll out dough to ¾ inch thick.
9. Cut using a 3-inch biscuit cutter.
10. Place on a cookie sheet 2 inches apart.
11. Bake for 15 minutes or until lightly brown.

Leila's Tasteful Tips:

- Use pecans or almonds instead of walnuts.
- Use figs or any other dried fruit instead of dates.

Chocolate Eggnog Scone Recipe

INGREDIENTS

4 cups of all-purpose Flour

2 large Eggs

¾ cup of Eggnog

6 Tablespoons unsalted Butter

2 teaspoons of ground Cinnamon

2 Tablespoons of Baking Powder

¼ teaspoon Salt

½ cup of granulated Sugar

2 Tablespoons of semi-sweet chocolate chips

DIRECTIONS

1. Preheat the oven to 350 degrees.
2. Line a baking sheet with parchment paper. Cut a second sheet of parchment paper to roll scones out.
3. In a large bowl mix dry ingredients (flour, sugar, baking powder, salt, and cinnamon) with a pastry cutter.
4. Cut butter into dry ingredients with the pastry cutter.
5. In a small bowl beat wet ingredients (eggs and eggnog) with a whisk.
6. Add wet ingredients to dry ingredients with the pastry cutter to incorporate.
7. Fold in chocolate chips.
8. Dust parchment paper with flour.
9. Cut dough in half.
10. Roll out to ½ inch thickness. Cut with a 3-inch biscuit cutter, putting scraps back into the bowl. Repeat until all the scones are cut out.
11. Makes 12 to 13 scones.
12. Bake for 10 to 15 minutes until scones are brown and solid to the touch.

Leila's Tasteful Tips:

- Instead of chocolate chips, cinnamon chips can be added.
- 2 Tablespoons of nuts such as walnuts or pecans can also be added.
- Dried cranberries can also be added for a fruity twist.

HOLIDAY SCONE TOPPERS

Leila's scones can stand on their own two feet! They do not need any enhancements and no toppings are needed. Even though you can not mess with perfection, scone toppers are commonplace in tea rooms and guests expect them.

Before tasting Leila's scones, guests smear devon cream on top. They ask for other toppings as well! It's just like salt. Some people put a huge amount of salt on their food even before taking a taste to see if salt is needed.

Leila puts much care in selecting the perfect dried fruits, chocolates or nuts that go into her perfect scones. A strawberry and devon cream make a cute Santa Hat (see the scone picture with the Santa hat). If you are interested in topping your scone, here are a few decadent add on options.

Chocolate Ganache
a Tasty, Chocolatey Topper

INGREDIENTS

1 12-ounce bag Milk Chocolate Chips

1 cup Heavy Cream

DIRECTIONS

1. Place the full bag of chocolate chips into a bowl and set aside.

2. Put heavy cream into a small saucepan. Bring to a boil. (Be careful the cream goes from cool to boil in minutes and can overflow very fast.)

3. Pour the boiled cream over the chocolate chips.

4. Using a whisk, continue to stir the chocolate until fully melted.

5. As the chocolate cools, it thickens.

Leila's Tasteful Tips:

- You can substitute the flavor of the chocolate chips to go with what you are making.

- You can add items to the chocolate mixture such as chopped nuts, crushed peppermint candy, or crushed cookies to make new flavor combinations.

Glaze
a Simple, Flavor Enhancer

INGREDIENTS

2 cups Powdered Sugar

1 teaspoon pure Vanilla Extract

¼ cup Heavy Cream

DIRECTIONS

1. Using a whisk, mix the above ingredients.

2. If needed, add additional heavy cream (a little at a time) to get your desired thickness.

Leila's Tasteful Tips:

- Change the extract to change the flavor. (Almond, Lemon and Orange)
- Reduce the heavy cream and add a syrup or preserves to change the flavor of the glaze. (Strawberry, Raspberry, Caramel, or Chocolate)

Peppermint Devon Cream
a Creamy burst of Mint

INGREDIENTS

3-ounces of Cream Cheese

2 Tablespoons Powdered Sugar

1 cup Heavy Cream

¼ cup crushed Peppermint Candy

DIRECTIONS

1. In a mixing bowl, using an electric hand mixer, combine the cream cheese and the sugar.

2. Beat in the heavy cream until thick.

3. Fold in the peppermint candy.

4. Refrigerate overnight.

Leila's Tasteful Tips:

- Use cold heavy cream in a cool space. It whips faster.

- You can add 1 teaspoon of your favorite extract to get the flavor of choice. Use the best flavor to enhance your scone flavor. (Vanilla, Almond, Lemon or Orange)

- For the best results, add the extract to the cream cheese and sugar mixture, before the heavy cream.

INSPIRED HOLIDAY DESSERTS

Inspiration comes from all around us. We never know where we are going to find the next inspired idea or in our instance the next great recipe. Leila and Erika gain new inspiration from movies, music and theater, people they meet on the street, and even with simple road signs during their road trips.

The other day, Leila went to a new doctor. His name was Dr. Michael Ricotta. Leila told him his name was very cute. He told Leila that his last name used to be Mozzarella from the famous Northern Italian Mozzarella family. He said he changed his name for business purposes. Leila said "Good change, Good change"!

Dr. Ricotta inspired Leila to create these fabulous Ricotta cookies. On Leila's next visit to Dr. Ricotta, she told him about these cookies and he was very excited. Leila explained that these cookies are cakelike cookies with a wonderful light and spongy taste. They are the perfect bite that takes the richness of ricotta and creates a delightfully soft, sweet treat that is perfect for a cozy afternoon tea or a festive gathering. Ricotta cookies were very popular in the Italian neighborhoods in Brooklyn, New York where Leila grew up. They are known as delicate clouds.

Ricotta is so versatile, it can be used in desserts as well as in main courses. Ricotta is the new Cream Cheese. Everytime we bake these cookies, they are devoured instantly. Trying to be "LadyLike" goes right out the door. Bake these for the Holidays and see what you think. You better make a bunch, because these cookie gems are going to fly into everyone's mouth.

Use your leftover Chocolate Ganache to dip one side of these Ricotta Cookies and then sprinkle with Holiday colored sugar. A dusting of powdered sugar will also add a snowy touch. These cookies can stand on their own, but make them picture perfect with these little enhancements!

One of Leila's favorite desserts is Tiramisu. The only thing she does not like is the wetness and taste of the alcohol used. Building her flavors with espresso chocolate chips and a chocolate hazelnut tea has her favorite Lady Finger Cookies dancing with a smile. Leila creates her Espresso Tiramisu with Holiday flair layering chocolate, cookies, and vanilla cream. It is Heaven on Earth and Goodwill to All!

Erika always says that you can't go wrong with cheesecake. This is one of her favorites. There are too many to list. For the Holidays, Leila tries to make all of Erika's favorites or else Erika reminds her that she was deprived. To make cheesecake a Holiday Star, Leila created her Raspberry Cheesecake Tarts. The Queen of Hearts called for these tarts and now will have no others!

There isn't a Christmas Holiday without fruitcake. Gingerbread Molasses Fruitcake Trees quickly became a cute tradition to the Erika's Tea Room menu. You will not hurt yourself lifting these soft, chewy delights, not typical of a fruitcake. Our Gingerbread tea adds great flavor, along with our Orange

Blossom Honey. This is an Erika tested and Leila approved recipe that now is a Holiday staple!

We all know liquor is quicker but candy is dandy. What is a Holiday without some Candy? Easy Christmas Swirl Fudge fills that need! Freshly made Fudge is soft, sweet and decadent. It hits all of the right Holiday notes!

Desserts are always the highlight of any meal, but Holiday desserts can make Memories that last a lifetime. With the inspiration we live by, "Memories Made with Every Cup", what goes best with a Holiday tea - a Holiday dessert - right? Let us share our favorite Holiday Dessert Recipes with you. They will add sweetness and joy to your Holiday Season!

HOLIDAY GLUTEN FREE DESSERTS

Just recently, Leila discovered the world of Almond Flour. When Leila learned to bake as a young girl, Almond Flour was not typically used. Certain desserts are gluten free, just because you use alternative gluten free flour. Now, Leila loves to experiment with new recipes that use Almond Flour adding a light, nutty flavor to new recipes. We all get those guests that just show up and then let us know that they are gluten free. Leila loves to be prepared by making the following recipes. We guarantee that no one will know that they are gluten free.

Leila was born in Brooklyn, New York surrounded by wonderful Italian Bakeries. One of their specialties was Italian Lace Cookies. These were served plain and chocolate dipped. Some had sprinkles on them. No one knew or even asked if they were gluten free. But, they were! They are the perfect light cookie served on the side of a perfect cup of tea!

How did Leila and Erika spend their summer vacation? In Arizona, in 130 degree weather! After a few days of melting, Leila asked Erika if she could find something indoors, air-conditioned to spend a few hours. Erika found a Macaron baking class. Leila was ecstatic. Leila and Erika baked French Macarons. Yes- even Erika made them and they came out perfectly! If Erika can bake - so can you!

Leila had tried to make macarons before, but did not succeed. After taking this class, Leila converted the recipe from grams to cups and created the recipe we attached. Leila played with great fillings and loves to share them with you. By the way, these Macarons are also gluten free! These gluten free recipes are so good that no one will know that they are gluten free!

Chocolate Chip Ricotta Cookies Recipe

INGREDIENTS

2 ½ cups all-purpose Flour

1 ½ teaspoons Baking Powder

½ teaspoon Baking Soda

1 ¼ cups granulated Sugar

1 cup (2 sticks) unsalted butter, melted

2 large Eggs

1 cup of Ricotta Cheese

½ teaspoon Salt

½ teaspoon pure Vanilla Extract

½ cup chopped Pistachios

1 cup mini semi-sweet Chocolate Chips

DIRECTIONS

1. Preheat the oven to 350 degrees.

2. In a medium bowl, whisk flour, baking powder, and baking soda.

3. In a large bowl, use an electric mixer to beat sugar and butter until fluffy and pale in color.

4. Add eggs, ricotta, salt, and vanilla.

5. Add dry ingredients and mix until dough forms.

6. Mix in pistachios and chocolate chips.

7. Refrigerate dough for 1 hour or more.

8. On a parchment lined baking sheet, roll dough into balls. Approximately 2 tablespoons. Space 2 inches apart on a baking sheet.

9. Bake for 12-14 minutes until the cookies are slightly golden brown and puffed. Rotate pan halfway through baking.

Leila's Tasteful Tips:

- Use ½ cup of macadamia nuts and 1 cup of white chocolate chips for a great flavor change.
- Press the dough balls down to make the cookies flatter.
- Or press a thumbprint in the middle of the dough ball and add a glazed cherry (red or green cherry) or a chocolate Hershey Kiss.

Espresso Tiramisu Recipe

INGREDIENTS

1 ½ cups of Heavy Cream, plus ½ cup of Heavy Cream for Ganache

8-ounces of Mascarpone Cheese

1/3 cup of granulated Sugar

1 teaspoon pure Vanilla Extract

2 cups of brewed Chocolate Hazelnut Tea

4 Tablespoons of Kahlua

2 packages of Lady Finger Cookies

6-ounce bag of espresso flavored Chocolate Chips

Espresso powder for dusting top

DIRECTIONS

1. Using an electric hand-mixer, combine heavy cream slowly adding sugar and vanilla until peaks form.

2. Fold in mascarpone. Put in the refrigerator until ready to use.

3. Ganache: Bring ½ cup of heavy cream to boil in a saucepan (Keep a close eye on the cream. It goes from cold to boiling in seconds.) Place espresso chocolate chips in a bowl, pour boiled cream over them, and whisk until smooth.

4. In a small bowl, combine Kahlua and the tea. (You can brew the tea ahead of time, so it can cool before dipping the cookies in it.)

5. Dip ladyfingers in the tea mixture. (Do not over-dip the cookie or it will fall apart.)

6. In a ½ sheet pan. Place dipped lady fingers side by side to cover the bottom of the pan.

7. Smooth ½ of the cheese mixture over the cookie layer.

8. Drizzle the ganache over the cheese mixture.

9. Make another full layer of dipped lady fingers.

10. Add the rest of the cheese mixture.

11. Sprinkle with Espresso Powder.

12. Drizzle with the remaining Ganache.

Leila's Tasteful Tips:

- You can make Strawberry Tiramisu by changing the Ganache to strawberry or white chocolate chips.
- Put fresh sliced strawberries between the cookie layers.

Raspberry Cheesecake Tarts Recipe

INGREDIENTS

1 stick unsalted Butter, melted

18 Graham Cracker sheets coarsely crushed

¾ of a cup plus 2 Tablespoons granulated Sugar

16-ounces whipped Cream Cheese

½ cup Sour Cream

½ teaspoon pure Vanilla Extract

¼ teaspoon Salt

2 large Eggs (lightly beaten)

1 18-ounce jar of seedless Raspberry Preserves

DIRECTIONS

1. Preheat the oven to 350 degrees.
2. Put graham crackers plus 2 Tablespoons of sugar in a food processor.
3. Stir in melted butter.
4. Press crumbs into the bottom of pans.
5. Bake the crust for 15 minutes and then cool.
6. Spread the full jar of the preserves evenly over the crust.
7. Reduce the oven to 325 degrees.
8. In a large bowl, beat with an electric hand-mixer, cream cheese and sour cream until smooth.
9. Add the ¾ cup of sugar, vanilla, and salt.
10. Add eggs and beat until smooth.
11. Pour cheese mixture over crust and bake for 25-35 minutes.
12. Chill for at least 1 hour or overnight.

Leila's Tasteful Tips:

- Change raspberry preserves for any flavor you prefer (cherry, strawberry, blackberry) or use a can of your favorite pie filling (apple, lemon, pumpkin)
- Instead of the preserves, use a 16-ounce container of Nutella and spread over the crust. Add ½ cup semi-sweet mini chocolate chips into cheese batter.

Gingerbread Molasses Fruit Cake Trees Recipe

INGREDIENTS CAKE

½ cup brewed Gingerbread Tea

2 Tablespoons dark Molasses

¾ cup Brown Sugar

1 ½ cups all-purpose Flour

½ teaspoon Baking Soda

½ teaspoon Salt

¾ teaspoon Cinnamon

½ teaspoon Baking Powder

¼ cup mixed glazed Fruit Peel

½ cup unsalted Butter (melted)

1 large Egg

INGREDIENTS GLAZE

½ teaspoon pure Vanilla Extract

½ teaspoon melted unsalted Butter

1 cup confectioners' Sugar

2 Tablespoons brewed Gingerbread Tea

DIRECTIONS

1. Preheat the oven to 350 degrees.

2. Using baking spray: Spray 2 of the Christmas Tree Pans.

3. In a small bowl: Put glazed fruit peel and hot tea. Add molasses and set aside. Cool.

4. In a medium bowl: whisk dry ingredients.

5. In a large bowl, use an electric hand-mixer: Mix butter, sugar, and eggs until fluffy.

6. Mix in dry ingredients to combine.

7. Add fruit peel mixture and beat well.

8. Spread batter into the well sprayed tree shaped trays.

9. Bake for 25 minutes.

10. Spread glaze immediately over trees. Let cool.

Leila's Tasteful Tips:

- Change the type of dried fruit as desired.
- Change the type of brewed tea for different seasonal treats.
- Change the baking pans to other shapes or make them in muffin liners.

Easy Christmas Swirl Fudge Recipe

INGREDIENTS

1 12-ounce bag of white chocolate chips

1 12-ounce tub creamy vanilla frosting

Green and Red gel food color

2 Tablespoons Christmas Sprinkles

DIRECTIONS

1. Line a 8-inch square pan with parchment paper (up the sides and press the corners to fit the pan).

2. Microwave white chocolate chips for 1 minute

3. Add frosting and microwave for 30 seconds.

4. Stir. Microwave for additional 15 second increments until smooth. Stir in between.

5. Split batter into 3 bowls.

6. Leave one white. Put 3 drops of red gel food color in the second batter. Put 3 drops of green gel food color in the third batter.

7. Put the white batter into the square pan. Drizzle in the first color. Using a knife marble through the white batter. Then drizzle in the last color and marble through the two colors.

8. Sprinkle Christmas sprinkles on the top.

9. Cover the pan with foil and refrigerate overnight.

10. To serve – cut fudge into small square pieces.

Leila's Tasteful Tips:

- Substitute milk chocolate chips, dark chocolate chips, or caramel chips for the white chocolate chips as desired.

- Substitute another flavor of frosting as desired.

- Add nuts such as slivered almonds or chopped pecans.

- Add dried fruit such as apricots, cherries or cranberries.

Holiday Gluten Free Desserts

We all get those guests that just show up and then let us know that they are gluten free. Be prepared by making the following recipes. We guarantee that no one will know that they are gluten free.

Almond Lace Cookie Recipe

INGREDIENTS

½ cup of unsalted Butter (8 Tablespoons or 1 Stick)

⅔ cup of packed Brown Sugar

¾ cup of Almond Flour

¼ teaspoons salt

1 Tablespoon light Corn Syrup

1 teaspoon pure Vanilla extract

DIRECTIONS

1. Preheat the oven to 350 degrees. Line 2 baking sheets with parchment paper.

2. In a medium saucepan on low heat, melt butter.

3. Add the brown sugar, almond flour, salt, and corn syrup with whisk.

4. Whisk until completely combined, approximately 3 to 4 minutes.

5. Remove the pan from the stove and whisk in vanilla. Mixture will be shiny and grainy.

6. Allow the cookie dough to rest 5 to 10 minutes and it will thicken.

7. Using a small cookie scoop or a teaspoon, place mixture 2 inches apart on cookie sheet. Flatten down the mixture slightly.

8. Bake for 7 minutes until golden brown around the edges.

9. Allow cookies to cool before adding the ganache. Store in a covered plastic container.

Leila's Tasteful Tips:

- Cookies can be served plain. They are delicious. To make them Holiday improved we are topping them with the Peppermint White Chocolate Ganache.

- These cookies stay fresh in a plastic container for two weeks. Just don't cover the cookies with the ganache until you are ready to serve them.

- Nutella is also a great center for a lace cookie sandwich.

Peppermint White Chocolate Ganache

INGREDIENTS

1 12-ounce bag White Chocolate Chips

¼ cup of crushed Peppermint Candy

1 cup Heavy Cream

DIRECTIONS

1. Place the full bag of chocolate chips into a bowl and set aside.

2. Put heavy cream into a small saucepan. Bring to a boil. (Be careful the cream goes from cool to boil in minutes and overflows very fast.)

3. Pour the boiled cream over the white chocolate chips.

4. Using a whisk, continue to stir the white chocolate chips until fully melted. Add the crushed peppermint candy.

5. As the chocolate cools, it thickens.

Peppermint Cream Cheese Frosting

INGREDIENTS

¼ cup crushed Peppermint Candy

1 16-ounce creamy Cream Cheese Frosting

DIRECTIONS

1. Mix the frosting and the peppermint candy.

Leila's Tasteful Tips:

- You can change the frosting for any flavor you like.
- Add ½ teaspoon of your favorite extract to make additional flavors.

Peppermint Cream Macarons Recipe

INGREDIENTS

1 ⅓ cups of Almond Flour

1 cup of Powdered Sugar

½ cup of Granulated Sugar

3 large Egg Whites (at room temperature, set on counter a couple of hours to age)

⅛ teaspoon Cream of Tartar

Green and Red Food Coloring Powder

EQUIPMENT

- Mesh Colander
- 2 Stainless Steel Mixing Bowls
- Spatula
- Cookie Sheet (lined with parchment paper)
- Kitchenaid Mixer (or other electric mixer)
- Disposable Piping Bag (16 or 18 inches)
- Wilton Round Tip #1A (for piping macarons)

DIRECTIONS

1. Separate 3 large eggs, putting egg whites aside to age. (Make sure you do not get any yolks into the whites.) Allow the egg whites to sit on the counter for at least 1 hour.

2. Preheat the oven to 350 degrees.

3. Place the colander over one of the mixing bowls.

4. First put the powdered sugar through the colander, then the almond flour. Set aside. (Use the spatula to push the sugar and flour through the sieve to sift.)

5. In the second mixing bowl measure out the granulated sugar. Set aside.

6. In the bowl of the electric mixer put the cream of tartar and the egg whites. Put the mixer on the first speed and beat until the egg whites are foamy.

7. Add ⅓ of the granulated sugar. Continue to whip the egg whites, adding another ⅓ and increasing the speed. It will look like cool whip with thick shiny peaks.

8. Remove bowl from mixer and add the flour and powdered sugar mixture ⅓ at a time, using the spatula. Add a small amount (pinch) of food coloring powder. (Fold the flour/sugar mixture into the egg whites until the batter is fully incorporated. A pinch of the food color goes a long way.)

9. Put the tip in the closed piping bag and fill with the batter. Cut the tip open.

10. Pipe quarter size circles 1 inch apart. (Make sure you pipe each the same size.)

11. Tap the baking tray on the counter to get rid of bubbles and set aside to dry (20 minutes) before baking.

12. Bake for 10 to 12 minutes.

13. Let macarons cool completely before removing them from the parchment paper.

14. In the middle of a set of macaron shells spread a teaspoon of the peppermint cream. (see recipe on page 109.)

Leila's Tasteful Tips:

- Some other great tasting fillings: Nutella, Peanut Butter and Jelly, or Lemon Curd.
- Add preserves to the frostings: Strawberry, Raspberry, or Fig.
- Put some dried fruit or nuts into the frosting.

HOLIDAY TEA TIME CRAFTS

What do you do with your guests after the food is gone and everyone is out-talked? Some fall asleep on the coach, pants open, in a sugar/food coma. Others watch sports or a Holiday movie or play a Holiday board game. Start a new Holiday tradition that will include everyone - a Holiday Craft Table.

We have many great tea time friends that live outside of Florida. We love to keep in touch with them, especially during Holiday time. We share scones and tea as we create different craft projects for our friends to collect and enjoy. A week before the craft event, the attendees receive a box with scones, tea, and everything needed to finish their project. Virtual Holiday tea time crafts can be shared with relatives and friends that are unable to be with you in person.

Leila prepares an example of each of these crafts before the event. Everyone wants to make a mirror-image of Leila's craft. Erika being the sales-lady extraordinaire sells Leila's craft before the event and often Leila has to make another one. Erika might be crafty in thought, but doesn't possess the skills to see it through! It's ok though, Erika comes up with great craft ideas for Leila to make!

The last Craft Event had the attendees cutting up a sock into 3 pieces. Even with Leila using chalk lines to show everyone where to cut the socks, it took much explaining to get the deed done. Are you one of those people who can take a pocket knife and q-tips into the wilderness and build a shopping mall? Let's see how crafty you are. Don't worry, below are step by step instructions to follow. These crafts will definitely get you into the Holiday spirit!

Holiday Tea Time Wreath

MATERIALS LIST

- Hot glue gun and glue sticks
- 10-inch foam ring
- 1 2-inch wide Holiday ribbon spool
- 12-inches solid red or Holiday ribbon
- 6 3-inch red pom poms
- 6 3-inch white pom poms
- 1 tea bag caddy
- 1 gold teacup charm

DIRECTIONS

1. Cover your foam ring with a wide Holiday ribbon.
2. Glue the end of the ribbon on the back of the ring.
3. Glue the pom poms to the wreath, alternating colors.
4. Take a thinner Holiday ribbon, tie the gold teacup charm to the tea bag caddy making a bow in the front.
5. Glue the tea bag caddy to the wreath.

Holiday Tea Time Angel

MATERIALS LIST

- Hot glue gun and glue sticks
- Holiday teacup
- 1 2-inch wood ball for the face
- Angel wings and halo
- 6-inches of pearl trim and a large faux pearl
- 1 heart-shaped rhinestone for the mouth
- 1 faux eyelash - cut in half for the eyes
- 1 1-inch by 3-inches faux fur piece for hair

DIRECTIONS

1. Take a Holiday bone china teacup and hold it upside down.
2. The ruffled base is the top of the Angel.
3. The teacup handle needs to be in the center and in the back of the Angel.
4. Glue the Angel wings to the handle, keeping the shiny side facing the front of the teacup.
5. Take the 3-inch wood ball and glue it to the ruffle base.
6. Glue the pearl trim to the teacup putting the large pearl in the center.
7. Glue the hair to the ball to create the Angel's head.
8. Cut the eyelash in half to make the Angel's eyes.
9. Glue on the heart gemstone for the Angel's mouth.
10. Glue on the gold Halo.

Holiday Tea Time Terrarium

MATERIALS LIST

- Hot glue gun and glue sticks
- Holiday teacup and saucer
- 1-inch of green foam
- Bag of cotton balls or white fluffy filler for the snow
- Miniature Holiday pieces (Santa, Snowman, Snowflakes, Presents, Rudolph, Trees)
- 2 miniature cardinals

DIRECTIONS

1. Take a Holiday teacup and glue it to the saucer, leaving the handle midway and to the right.
2. Glue a piece of foam inside the teacup.
3. Glue the snow to the foam and coming down the saucer.
4. Use miniature Holiday pieces to make your scene (Santa, Snowman, Snowflakes, Presents, Rudolph, Trees).
5. Put a miniature cardinal on the teacup handle and another one on the teacup top.

ERIKA'S TEA ROOM 3-DAY RETREAT

As Erika's Tea Room continues to grow and expand their footprint, Leila and Erika strive to have new and exciting ways to interact with their customers and continue to build lifelong relationships. Erika chats with customers on the phone who long to visit the tea room in person. It would be wonderful to put faces with familiar voices. We were inspired to create a brand new 3-day Retreat!

People love tea, they love crafts, they love food and they love learning to cook and bake. Put it all together and what have you got: a wonderful fun-packed 3-day retreat. If you want to be in the now, "Retreats" are the in thing! It comes from the saying "treat yourself to something special and unique, "You" deserve it!

How do you pack all that we do into just 3-days? We've created an immersive program that tickles your taste buds, gets your creative juices flowing, and just makes you happy. From tasting teas from all over the world, to creating your own custom tea blends, sampling Matcha tea in many flavors and a flight of iced teas all will experience the unique varieties of tea.

Of course, tea must have the perfect food pairing. In the tea room we combine our wonderful menus with Murder Mysteries, Themed Events, and Holiday High Tea Menus. Whether you are an experienced cook and baker or a novice, Leila will demonstrate some of her favorite Holiday recipes. We will bring you into Leila's kitchen and learn to bake some of her tea time sweets. In the kitchen,

Leila will share her tips and tricks to cook her favorite tea time foods. Of course, many samples will be provided to get the full experience.

Honey tasting, charcuterie, bread baking, pickling and other activities will pack the day with lots of fun. Attendees will be able to ask questions and gain insight in everything that Erika's Tea Room offers. A copy of the latest Erika's Tea Room cookbook will be given to each guest to take home and recreate recipes in their own kitchens.

The Retreat Agenda includes a morning and afternoon break. In our first retreat, these breaks were the perfect time to shop for all their tea time treasures to take home. It is the best time to do Holiday shopping under one roof, with Erika as your personal shopping guide. She is the one to help you find the perfect gift!

Leila and Erika continue to look forward to creating new and exciting Retreat ideas. They are cultivating a new Spring 3-day retreat. Not to give much away, but Bunnies seem to be a primary focus. Many new recipes are underdevelopment and will be included in our next cookbook. Some of which will be offered in the Retreat. Fantastic tea time craft ideas are under discussion. Everything is hush hush, as we make our list and check it twice! Leila and Erika can not wait to see all of our tea time friends in one or more of our Retreats very soon!

HOLIDAY CHARCUTERIE BOARDS

When the family comes to call they walk in hungry and ready to eat. What you have prepared might not yet be ready to serve, so a Holiday Charcuterie Board is an attractive and tasty alternative to appetizers. Charcuterie boards are all the rage right now! With a variety of meats, cheeses, fruits and nuts, olives and gherkins, and breads, these Holiday Charcuterie Boards also known as "Grazing Boards" are perfect for serving at your Christmas party this year!

Don't forget a flair of your own to your special Holiday Charcuterie. Add dips and spreads in small ramekins strategically placed next to items that they go along with. These spreads can be condiments such as mustard, honey or jam, or be as intricate as fruit dips, homemade hummus, or liver pates. Mix dried fruits with fresh fruits smattered around the board. Lastly, bread items act as vessels to get every drop of prepared items into your mouth, a shovel if you will! These bread items can be as simple as crackers or bread sticks or as distinct as cut out and toasted bread flowers and bread cups using various types of bread.

By making smaller Holiday Charcuterie Boards you can separate the various themes of items included. The Classic Meat and Cheese Charcuterie Board includes cured meats and pates, sliced or cubed cheeses, and crackers or breads. Add a condiment or two to complete this board. The Dessert Charcuterie Board includes fresh fruits, dried fruits, chocolates, small cakes or cookies, and nuts. Add a fruit dip or glaze for dipping to elevate the provisions on this board. Another Holiday Charcuterie Board could be for the Vegetarians in your life, or just those guests who love veggies. You can place fresh vegetables (cucumber slices, cherry tomatoes, carrot sticks, raw broccoli and cauliflower, slices of red, green, and yellow peppers) and marinated vegetables (mushrooms, roasted red peppers, olives, and pickles) on the board. Add a homemade dressing or aioli for dipping.

A Holiday Charcuterie is a tasty alternative to traditional appetizers, a salad course, or an addition to dessert. As an appetizer a Wreath, a Candy Cane or a Christmas Tree shaped wooden board is perfect to make a Bruschetta Caprese Charcuterie. By overlapping fresh slices of mozzarella cheese with thinly sliced tomatoes, fresh basil as leaves, and occasional slices of roasted red peppers; your Holiday appetizer is finished. Or add a little spice to your life by including an occasional slice of pepperoni. Add a drizzle of extra virgin olive oil and a thick balsamic vinegar to complete this dish.

Using a Lazy Susan as your canvas, lay individual lettuce cups as your base covering the entire surface. Peel and dice an English cucumber, a tomato, and a red onion. Put even amounts in each lettuce cup. Sprinkle each cup with cooked crispy bacon and a teaspoon of your favorite prepared dressing.

Dessert Charcuterie finishes a Holiday meal in style and grace. Choose a long, narrow Charcuterie board. Make skewers of fresh or dried fruits, chunks of cheese, chunks of pound cake, small marshmallows, and soft small cookies. Alternate the skewers on the board. These will wow your guests.

First there were small plates, now there is Charcuterie!

Simple Holiday Fruit Dip Recipe

INGREDIENTS

32-ounce container of Vanilla flavored Greek Yogurt

8-ounce Cool Whip Topping (thawed)

1 3.4-ounce box of instant Vanilla Pudding

DIRECTIONS

1. Using an electric hand mixer, mix yogurt and pudding until well combined.
2. Fold in thawed cool whip topping.
3. Refrigerate overnight.

Leila's Tasteful Tips:

- Change the flavor of the yogurt to a fruit one such as Strawberry to change the taste.
- Use a 16-ounce container of sour cream instead of the yogurt.

Holiday Guacamole Dip Recipe

INGREDIENTS

1 8-ounce container of Mild Classic Guacamole

¼ cup of Mayonnaise

2 Tablespoons of Sour Cream

1 teaspoon of pure Lime Juice

1 teaspoon of ground Black Pepper

1 teaspoon of Garlic Powder

1 teaspoon of Onion Powder

1 Tablespoon of dried Chives

DIRECTIONS

1. In a large mixing bowl, combine all the ingredients.
2. Refrigerate overnight.

Leila's Tasteful Tips

- Add canned diced tomatoes (drained).
- Add 2 Tablespoons of finely diced red onions.

HOLIDAY CHARCUTERIE TEACUP

Holiday season is totally tea season. Adorable Holiday Charcuterie Teacups that are filled with fruits, cheeses, crackers and nuts are the perfect food or snack idea for Holiday tea parties and celebrations.

To prepare an elegant Holiday Luncheon, individual Holiday Charcuterie Teacups with a Holiday flavor cuppa tea elevates your Holiday celebration. It is the perfect way to wow your guests and make them feel special.

Charcuterie Teacups are so easy and fun to make. Once you gather up some gorgeous Holiday teacups, it's time to add some goodies to them.

These mini masterpieces are the perfect blend of convenience and creativity. Start off by putting some nuts on the bottom of the teacup. They will help keep everything else in place. There are usually special spiced nuts available during the Holiday Season. Choose a meat flower or a meat rollup or both for your guests.

Next, make your skewers. Cheese chucks, meat, and olives on one skewer. Then, fruits and marinated cheese balls, and vegetable sticks on another. Breadsticks and a large cracker or two are also added. Dried fruits, as well as a few berries can be scattered along the base of the teacup.

Bread flowers make an adorable Holiday topper for your skewer.

Holiday Bread Flowers Recipe

INGREDIENTS

1 package fresh Bread (multigrain, honey wheat, butter, Hawaiian)

1-inch holiday Cookie Cutter

2 Tablespoons of unsalted Butter (melted)

1 teaspoon of Garlic Powder

DIRECTIONS

1. Preheat the oven to 350 degrees.
2. Cut out the shape from your favorite fresh bread.
3. Melt 2 tablespoons of unsalted butter. Add garlic powder.
4. Lightly brush bread with butter.
5. Bake for 7 minutes until lightly browned.
6. Place on the tips of finished skewers.

Leila's Tasteful Tips:

- Do not over bake the bread flowers or they will get hard.
- You can make the bread flowers in advance. When cool, store in a sealed plastic container. Lasts up to a week on the counter.
- Use various shapes of Holiday cookie cutters to make your charcuterie teacups very festive. (i.e. Star, Tree, Snowflake, or Bell)

OUR FUTURE CONTINUES, WHAT TO EXPECT IN THE CHAPTERS TO COME

Who can say what will happen next? We polish our crystal ball and see the obvious. Leila and Erika are hand in hand planning, changing, and creating something shiny and new. We know there will always be new recipes, new crafts, new cooking and demonstrations, new events, and much much more in Erika's Tea Room's future.

We would love to see some recognition for what we do come our way. Recognition or not, we love what we do and will continue doing it into the distant future. Things will change, since change is inevitable. We learned early on that changing on a dime is necessary for Erika's Tea Room's survival.

When Leila and Erika put their heads together, they can accomplish anything. The Moon and the Stars are no longer out of reach. Erika knows that we will continue to offer themed events and special Holiday tea time meals. Leila will continue to teach anyone who asks about cooking and baking and show them what is beyond the recipes. Erika will create new Scone and Gift Bundles to keep tea lovers motivated. Leila will feed all guests entering the tea room doors and not let anyone leave hungry.

So, everyone raise your tea cup because we continually wish you, our tea room family and friends - good scones, good food, good tea and especially good "Memories Made with Every Cup!"

www.ingramcontent.com/pod-product-compliance
Lightning Source LLC
Chambersburg PA
CBRC091800090426
42811CB00021B/1900